Human Dignity, Sexuality, and Marriage & Family

THE CATHOLIC FAITH SERIES

Volume Three

D0899544

Libreria Editrice Vaticana

United States Conference of Catholic Bishops
Washington, DC

ISBN 978-1-60137-339-7

First printing, December 2012

Contents

Preface

How did the project for this book come about?

For about three years, I have been placing in the Basilica of San Carlo al Corso (Rome), of which I am rector, some catechetical pamphlets on topics related to current events, available to anyone who comes into the basilica. And to my surprise I noticed that more than 2.5 million pamphlets have been taken by people passing through the basilica. So in response to the demand from so many people, I decided to collect, in a compact and portable format, the pamphlets in question.

What criterion was used to select the topics?

The criterion of relevance. I decided to present brief summaries of what the Catholic Church teaches about some of the timely topics that are being brought to people's attention now for various reasons. In some cases I have also tried to select topics that are somewhat forgotten by many Christians today, or even disputed by some of them.

What documents were used in addressing these topics?

Mainly the documents of the Holy See, and for two reasons. First, because these documents tend to be overlooked by the general public, and their richness, comprehensiveness, and beauty deserve to be more widely known. Second, because they express essential and fundamental beliefs that are held not by any one Catholic alone, but by the Catholic Church as a whole, transmitted through the Magisterium of the pope and the bishops. This Magisterium was established by Christ himself, to confirm the faith of individual believers in him so that down through the centuries and in various parts of the world all may profess one and the same Catholic faith.

Why are the topics presented in dialogue form?

From an editorial point of view, the topics are presented in the form of a dialogue, with questions followed by briefly summarized answers.

This dialogue form tends to be more inviting for the reader, and also continues a constant and long-standing catechetical tradition in the history of the Church. Many catechisms that have formed entire generations have used, and very fruitfully, this didactical system of question and answer.

It must also not be forgotten that the Christian faith itself, a special gift from God, is a continual dialogue of God with man, and of man with God.

I also think that it corresponds to the needs of the contemporary world, in which journalistic-style interviews are preferred, as well as summarized formulations, partly because of the little time that many people, even those who identify themselves as Catholic, now set aside for the catechetical study of their own faith. And this lack of time unfortunately leads to religious ignorance, which in turn leads to widespread relativism, to an arbitrary subjectivism, and last but not least to a distressing vacuum of knowledge about the contents of the faith, which characterizes not only children and young people in their catechetical journey but also adults in their varied and demanding activities.

What is the purpose of this book?

It may help people to understand better the beauty and the importance of the response that the Christian faith offers to all on some topics that characterize our society even today.

This book contains only some of the elements that make up the rich and mysterious panorama of the Catholic faith, and only some of the problems that are eating away at the world today. At the same time, I want to emphasize that in dealing with the individual topics, I do not intend to present all of their aspects and elements, and therefore I do not mean to give each argument exhaustive and complete treatment, but to offer only a few thoughts, fragments of reflection.

So it is intended both for Christians, whom it may provide with an opportunity for a better and deeper understanding of the elements of their faith, and for anyone who might wish to know what the Catholic Church, through some of its official documents, believes and lives, with the help of God.

His Excellency Raffaello Martinelli
Bishop of Frascati
Frascati, September 12, 2010
First anniversary of my episcopal ordination

I
In the Image
of God

What is the basis of the statement that "I am created in the image of God"?

It is based in the Bible. Right in its first pages, in fact, we read: "God created mankind in his image; / in the image of God he created them; / male and female he created them" (Gn 1:27).

When do human beings begin to be in the image of God?

They begin at the first moment of conception. This dignity is therefore present at every stage of human life, which is an inalienable and indispensable good. The Church proclaims this truth not only with the authority of the Gospel but also with the persuasion of reason, and precisely for this reason feels the duty to appeal to all people of good will, in the certainty that accepting this truth can only benefit individuals and society.

How does being in the image of God come to human beings?

✠   It comes from God. It is God himself who gives this special gift to human beings, who receive it gratuitously. It is therefore not a human achievement.

✠   Human beings have a responsibility

- To recognize this gift
- To thank the Giver, God
- To manifest and increase in their lives the fruits of this gift
- To bear witness courageously, in their everyday actions, to being in the image of God

What does it mean that God has created us in his image?

✠   Saying that God has created us in his image means that

- He wanted each one of us to manifest an aspect of his infinite splendor
- He has a plan for each one of us
- Each one of us is destined to enter, through a journey that is individual for each one, into eternal beatitude. The creature is therefore in the image of God precisely because of the fact that it participates in immortality, not by nature, but as a gift of the Creator.

Orientation to eternal life is what makes the human person become the corresponding creature of God.

✠ "Human dignity is not something that presents itself to our view, it is not measurable or describable, it evades the parameters of scientific or technical reason; but our civilization, our humanism, has made no progress except to the extent to which this dignity has been more universally and more permanently recognized by more and more people" (Cardinal Joseph Ratzinger, Address to the Pontifical Council for Pastoral Assistance to Health Care Workers, November 28, 1996).

✠ "If you say, 'Show me your God,' I will say to you, 'Show me the man who is in you, and I will show you my God'" (St. Theophilus of Antioch, *Apologia to Autolycus*).

In what sense are human beings created "in the image of God"?

✠ "The human person is created in the image of God in the sense that he or she is capable of knowing and of loving their Creator in freedom. Human beings are the only creatures on earth that God has willed for their own sake and has called to share, through knowledge and love, in his own divine life. All human beings, in as much as they are created in the image of God, have the dignity of a person. A person is not something but someone, capable of self-knowledge and of freely giving himself and entering into communion with God and with other persons" (*Compendium of the Catechism of the Catholic Church* [*Compendium of the CCC*], no. 66).

✠ "More specifically, the human person is the image of God because of at least six characteristics:

1. Rationality, or the capacity to know and comprehend the created world
2. Freedom, which implies the capacity and the duty to decide, and responsibility for the decisions made (see Gn 2)
3. A position of authority, but in no way absolute, rather under the dominion of God
4. The capacity to act in conformity with the one in whose image the human person is, meaning to imitate God
5. The dignity of being a person, a 'relational' being, capable of having personal relationships with God and with other human beings (see Gn 2)
6. The sanctity of human life" (Pontifical Biblical Commission, *Bibbia e morale* [Libreria Editrice Vaticana (LEV), 2008], 17-18)

✠ "The strongest proof that we are made in the image of the Trinity is this: love alone makes us happy because we live in a relationship, and we live to love and to be loved. Borrowing an analogy from biology, we could say that imprinted upon his 'genome,' the human being bears a profound mark of the Trinity, of God as Love" (Pope Benedict XVI, *Angelus*, June 7, 2009).

What dimensions of the person are involved in being created in the image of God?

✠ All of the person is involved, and every person.

✠ In particular, his or her

- Dignity
- Unity of body and soul
- Being man or woman
- Relationship with God, with self, with others, with the world

✠ It is therefore the person as a whole who is created in the image of God. "Without the Creator the creature would disappear" (*Gaudium et Spes*, no. 36). The Bible presents a vision of the human being in which the spiritual dimension is seen together with the physical, social, and historical dimension.

In what way does being in the image of God involve human dignity?

✠ It involves human dignity in that it is the foundation of this. Human beings find the foundation of their dignity precisely in being created in the image of God.

✠ In fact, human dignity

- Is not based on genetics
- Does not depend on possessions or abilities, much less on race, culture, or nationality

- Is not diminished by physical differences or genetic defects

✠ The foundation of the full and authentic dignity inherent in every person lies in the fact that he or she is created in the image and likeness of God. "The dignity of the human person is rooted in his or her creation in the image and likeness of God. Endowed with a spiritual and immortal soul, intelligence and free will, the human person is ordered to God and called in soul and in body to eternal beatitude" (*Compendium of the* CCC, no. 358).

✠ Founded in this way, human dignity distinguishes the person in an essential way from all other created beings (this is referred to as an "ontological difference"—on the level of being, and not simply on the functional level of action—between human beings and the rest of the world). The Bible emphasizes this difference in its very first pages, where it says that after the creation of the things of this world, "God saw that it was good" (Gn 1:25), but after the creation of human beings, "God looked at everything he had made, and found it very good" (Gn 1:31).

What is the relationship between being in the image of God and being in communion with God?

✠ Being created in the image of God is the foundation of the orientation of the human person to God. It is precisely this radical resemblance to the One and Triune God that is the basis of the possibility for the human person to enter into communion with the Most Holy Trinity.

This is what God himself wanted. In fact, the One and Triune God wanted to share his Trinitarian communion with persons created in his image. It was for this Trinitarian communion that the human person was created in the image of God. The purpose of the human person is therefore to know, love, and serve him in this life, and to enjoy him in the next, and to love one's neighbor as God does.

✠ "Created 'in the image of God,' man also expresses the truth of his relationship with God the Creator by the beauty of his artistic works" (*Catechism of the Catholic Church* [CCC], no. 2501).

Does the body also participate in this image of God?

✠ Yes, the body itself, as an intrinsic part of the person, participates in his or her creation in the image of God.

✠ In the Christian faith

- It is the soul that is created in the image of God.
- Since the soul is the *substantial form* of the body, the human person as a whole is the bearer of the divine image in a dimension that is just as physical as it is spiritual.
- The human person does not merely *have* a body, but *is* also the body.
- Body-soul dualism is therefore excluded.
- The person is considered as a whole, in unity: as an incarnate spirit, a soul that expresses itself in the body and a body informed by an immortal spirit.

- Physicality is therefore essential to personal identity.
- The affirmation of the resurrection of the body at the end of the world makes it clear that even in eternity the human being is a complete physical and spiritual person.

✠ The Christian faith therefore clearly affirms the unity of the human being and understands physicality as essential to personal identity, both in this life and in the next.

Why is the image of God also manifested in the difference of the sexes?

✠ Because the human being exists only as male or female, and this sexual difference, far from being an accidental or secondary aspect of the personality, is an essential element of personal identity. So the sexual dimension also belongs to being in the image of God. Man and woman are equally created in the image of God, each of them in a unique and special way. This is why the Christian faith speaks of reciprocity and complementarity between the sexes.

✠ Created in the image of God, human beings are created for love and communion. Because this vocation is realized in a special way in the unitive and procreative union between husband and wife, the difference between man and woman is an essential element of the constitution of human beings made in the image of God. "God created mankind in his image; in the image of God he created them; male and female he created them" (Gn 1:27; see Gn 5:1-2). According to Scripture, therefore, the *imago Dei* is in part manifested, from the very beginning, in the difference between the sexes.

✠ "Sexuality affects all aspects of the human person in the unity of his body and soul. It especially concerns affectivity, the capacity to love and to procreate, and in a more general way the aptitude for forming bonds of communion with others" (CCC, no. 2332).

✠ The roles attributed to one sex or the other can vary over time and space, but the sexual identity of the person is not a cultural or social construct. It belongs to the specific way in which the *imago Dei* exists.

✠ This sexual specificity is reinforced by the Incarnation of the Word. He took on the human condition in its totality, assuming one sex, but becoming man in both senses of the term: as a member of the human community, and as a being of the masculine sex (see International Theological Commission [ITC], *Communion and Stewardship: Human Persons Created in the Image of God*, no. 34).

✠ Moreover, the Incarnation of the Son of God and the resurrection of the body at the end of time also extend into eternity the original sexual identity of the *imago Dei*.

Why does being in the image of God also involve our relationship with other persons?

✠ Precisely because God is Trinity, a communion of three Persons in the one divine nature, the person too, created in the image of God, is therefore capable of being in relationship with other persons, a being who

- Has a fundamental orientation toward other persons
- Is called to form a community with them

✠ "It follows that personal beings are social beings as well. The human being is truly human to the extent that he actualizes the essentially social element in his constitution as a person within familial, religious, civil, professional, and other groups that together form the surrounding society to which he belongs" (*Communion and Stewardship*, no. 42).

✠ Marriage constitutes an elevated form of communion between human persons, and one of the best analogies of the Trinitarian life. "The prime instance of this communion is the procreative union of man and woman which mirrors the creative communion of Trinitarian love" (*Communion and Stewardship*, no. 56). When a man and a woman unite their bodies and spirits in an attitude of total openness and self-giving, they form a new image of God. Their union in one flesh does not respond simply to a biological necessity, but to the intention of the Creator, which leads to sharing the happiness of being made in his image (see CCC, no. 2331).

✠ Humanity itself, in its original unity (which Adam symbolizes), is made in the image of the divine Trinity.
    "All people form the unity of the human race by reason of the common origin which they have from God. God has made 'from one ancestor all the nations of men' (Acts 17:26).

All have but one Savior and are called to share in the eternal happiness of God" (*Compendium of the* CCC, no. 68).

How does being in the image of God also involve our relationship with created things?

Being created in the image of God is the foundation of

- Our relationship with created things
- Our superiority over the visible world. The human person is the summit of the visible creation, as the only being created in the image and likeness of God.
- Our participation in the divine rule over creation

In what way does the human person participate in the sovereignty of God over the world?

✠ Participating in the sovereignty of God over the world means that the human person

- Exercises this sovereignty over the visible creation only by virtue of the privilege to do so that is granted by God
- Recognizes God as the Creator of all, gives him thanks and praise for the gift of creation, glorifying the name of God
- Is not the supreme lord over the world. God, the Creator of the world, is the Lord par excellence over the world. The human person is a subordinate lord (with a ministerial and subordinate sovereignty).

- Is designated by God to be his collaborator, tenant, and administrator. The human person is called by God to exercise, in the name of God himself, a responsible administration over the created world. This administration "is limited by concern for the quality of life of his neighbor, including generations to come; it requires a religious respect for the integrity of creation" (CCC, no. 2415).
- As an administrator, must render an account for his or her actions, which will be judged by God

✠ This sovereignty is exercised in respect for creation. The human person, as an image of God, does not dominate over the world. Human administration of the created world is a service carried out through participation in the divine rule. "Human beings exercise this stewardship by gaining scientific understanding of the universe, by caring responsibly for the natural world (including animals and the environment), and by guarding their own biological integrity" (*Communion and Stewardship*, no. 61).

✠ Human work itself "proceeds directly from persons created in the image of God and called to prolong the work of creation by subduing the earth, both with and for one another" (CCC, no. 2427), collaborating with God the Creator.

What is the relationship between being in the image of God and the natural law?

In creating the human person in his image, God has placed in the depths of the human conscience a law, which "the tradition calls the 'natural law.' This law is of divine origin, and man's awareness of it is itself a participation in the divine law" (*Communion and Stewardship*, no. 60).

The natural law is the light of reason infused into the human heart by God. It is therefore a law within the person, engraved in the soul and able to be known by all through reason. Of a universal character, it precedes and unites all rights and duties, being a common denominator for all persons and all peoples. And the *Compendium of the CCC* affirms in this regard: "The natural law which is inscribed by the Creator on the heart of every person consists in a participation in the wisdom and the goodness of God. It expresses that original moral sense which enables one to discern by reason the good and the bad. It is universal and immutable and determines the basis of the duties and fundamental rights of the person as well as those of the human community and civil law" (no. 416). It "constitutes the true guarantee offered to each one to live in freedom and in the respect for his dignity as a person, and to feel protected from any ideological manipulation and from all abuse perpetrated based on the law of the strongest" (Pope Benedict XVI, Address to the ITC, December 5, 2008).

Is this law perceived by all?

"Because of sin the natural law is not always perceived nor is it recognized by everyone with equal clarity and immediacy.

"For this reason God 'wrote on the tables of the Law what men did not read in their hearts' (St. Augustine)" (*Compendium of the CCC*, no. 417).

How is being in the image of God affected by sin?

✠ Sin does not destroy, it does not erase the image of God in the human person. The human person is an image of God by virtue of being a person and remains so as long as life endures. The divine image is connected to the human essence as such, and it is not in the power of human beings to destroy it completely.

✠ Sin, depending on its objective gravity and on the subjective responsibility of the person, disfigures the image of God in the person, it wounds and obscures it. And precisely because sin is like a wound in the image of God in the person, it also wounds and obscures the person

- In his or her dignity, causing an inner division between body and spirit, knowledge and will, reason and emotion
- In his or her relationship with God, with self, with others, with creation

✠ Wounded by sin, the human person is in need of salvation. And God, who is infinitely good, offers this salvation in nothing less than his Only Begotten Son Jesus Christ, who heals and frees the human person through his Death and Resurrection.

✠ The disfigurement of the image of God by sin, with its inevitable negative consequences for personal and interpersonal life, is therefore overcome by the Passion, Death, and Resurrection of Christ.

What model does the human person have for living in the image of God?

✠ In the first place, the human person understands himself or herself, and above all the reality of being in the image of God, only in the light of Christ. "The truth is that only in the mystery of the incarnate Word does the mystery of man take on light. For Adam, the first man, was a figure of Him who was to come, namely, Christ the Lord. Christ, the final Adam, by the revelation of the mystery of the Father and His love, fully reveals man to man himself and makes his supreme calling clear" (*Gaudium et Spes*, no. 22). The mystery of the human person is clarified only in the light of Christ, who is the perfect image "of the invisible God, the firstborn of all creation" (Col 1:15), and who through the Holy Spirit makes us participants in the mystery of the One and Triune God. "Thus, what it means to be created in the *imago Dei* is only fully revealed to us in the *imago Christi*" (*Communion and Stewardship*, no. 53).

✠ God the Father calls us to be "conformed to the image of his Son" (Rom 8:29) through the work of the Holy Spirit. "The Holy Spirit works mysteriously in all human beings of good will, in societies and in the cosmos to transfigure and divinize human beings. Moreover, the Holy Spirit works through all the sacraments, particularly the Eucharist" (Communion and Stewardship, no. 54).

✠ Through the Holy Spirit, "the saving grace of participation in the paschal mystery reconfigures the *imago Dei* according to the pattern of the *imago Christi* . . . In this way, man's everyday existence is defined as an endeavor to be conformed ever more fully to the image of Christ and to dedicate his life to the struggle to bring about the final victory of Christ in the world" (*Communion and Stewardship*, nos. 56, 55). So we become fully in the image of God by participating in divine life in Christ.

In what way is Christ the model for every person on how to live in the image of God?

✠ The original image of the person, who in turn represents the image of God, is Christ, and the person is created on the basis of the image of Christ, in his image. The human being is at the same time a preliminary design in view of Christ; or rather, Christ is the perfect and fundamental image of the Creator, and God forms the human being precisely in view of him, his Son.

✠ The possibilities that Christ opens for the human person do not signify the suppression of the reality of the person as creature, but his or her transformation and realization according to the perfect image of the Son.

✠ At the same time, there is tension between the concealment and the future manifestation of the image of God. Here we can apply the words from the first Letter of John, "We are God's children now; what we shall be has not yet been revealed" (1 Jn 3:2).

All human beings are already in the image of God, in the image of Christ, even though it has not yet been revealed what they will become at the end of time, when the Lord Jesus will come on the clouds of heaven, so that God "may be all in all" (1 Cor 15:28). The *imago Dei* can therefore be considered, in a real way, something dynamic that is still taking shape.

✠ Our conformity to the image of Christ is therefore perfectly fulfilled only at our Resurrection at the end of time, in which Christ has gone before us, taking with him his Mother, Mary Most Holy.

In what sense can it also be said that God is in our image?

In a twofold sense:

- "We are your image, and you our image through the union that you have established between yourself and humanity, concealing your eternal divinity in the poor cloud of the corrupt humanity of Adam. For what reason? Love, of course" (St. Catherine of Siena, *Dialogue of Divine Providence*, ch. 13).
- The Son of God, consubstantial with the Father according to his divinity, in becoming man, has taken on our human nature, becoming consubstantial with us according to his humanity, "similarly . . . tested in every way, yet without sin" (Heb 4:15).

II
Human Rights

What are the international conventions on human rights?

Here are the main international conventions:

✠ The *Universal Declaration of Human Rights*, adopted by the United Nations on December 10, 1948:

- John Paul II called it "a real milestone on the path of the moral progress of humanity" (Address to the 34th General Assembly of the United Nations, October 2, 1979); a point of arrival, but also a point of departure.
- The precursor and inspiration for this declaration was a Dominican friar, the Spanish philosopher and theologian Francisco de Vitoria (1483-1546), who made an extensive contribution to the preparation of the *Charter of Rights of the Indians*. This was aimed at protecting the rights of indigenous peoples during the conquest of the Americas.
- The human rights that are proclaimed in the aforementioned declaration are an expression of the eminent

and inviolable dignity of every human person, manifesting his or her unique and unrepeatable vocation, beyond any sort of difference and any discrimination.

✠ The *Declaration of the Rights of the Child* (1959) states that "the child, for the full and harmonious development of his personality, needs love and understanding. He shall, wherever possible, grow up in the care and under the responsibility of his parents."

✠ The *Convention on the Elimination of All Forms of Racial Discrimination* (1965) condemns all racist theory and practice and commits the member nations to fighting against the forms of prejudice that lead to racial discrimination.

✠ The *International Covenant on Economic, Social and Cultural Rights* (1966) affirms that "the widest possible protection and assistance should be accorded to the family, which is the natural and fundamental group unit of society, particularly for its establishment and while it is responsible for the care and education of dependent children" (Article 10).

What are the fundamental human rights?

✠ The *Universal Declaration of Human Rights* indicates the following in particular: all human beings are born free and equal (art. 1). They have the right to life, liberty, and security (art. 3). No individual may be kept in a state of slavery (art. 4), nor may anyone be subjected to torture or to cruel and inhuman punishment (art. 5). Everyone has the right to recognition as a person before the law (art. 6). All are equal before the law (art. 7). No individual may be arbitrarily arrested, detained, or exiled (art. 9). Every accused person is to be presumed innocent until proven guilty (art. 11). Everyone has the right to freedom of movement and residence (art. 13) and to citizenship (art. 15). Men and women have equal rights with regard to marriage (art. 16). Everyone has the right to personal property (art. 17), to freedom of thought, conscience, and religion (art. 18), of opinion and expression (art. 19), to peaceful assembly (art. 20), and to participate in the government of one's country (art. 21).

✠ John Paul II outlined a list of human rights in the encyclical *Centesimus Annus*, where it is affirmed that every human being has the right

- To life, an integral part of which is the right of the child to develop in the mother's womb from the moment of conception
- To live in a united family and in a moral environment conducive to the growth of the child's personality
- To develop one's intelligence and freedom in seeking and knowing the truth
- To share in the work which makes wise use of the earth's material resources, and to derive from that work the means to support oneself and one's dependents
- Freely to establish a family, to have and to rear children through the responsible exercise of one's sexuality

"In a certain sense, the source and synthesis of these rights is religious freedom" (no. 47), which is also the foundational element for all liberties, the ultimate criterion of their protection, the guarantee of authentic pluralism and true democracy.

What is the scope of religious freedom?

Religious freedom must be understood, promoted, and defended "in all its dimensions, including ritual, worship, education, dissemination of information and the freedom to profess and choose religion. It is inconceivable, then, that believers should have to suppress a part of themselves—their faith—in order to be active citizens. It should never be necessary to deny God in order to enjoy one's rights . . . The full guarantee of religious liberty cannot be limited to the free exercise of worship, but has to give due consideration to the public dimension of religion, and hence to the possibility of believers playing their part in building the social order . . . Human rights, of course, must include the right to religious freedom, understood as the expression of a dimension that is at once individual and communitarian—a vision that brings out the unity of the person while clearly distinguishing between the dimension of the citizen and that of the believer" (Pope Benedict XVI, Address to the General Assembly of the United Nations, April 18, 2008).

What is the foundation of human rights?

✠ Human rights do not have their foundation

- Solely in the will of human beings. This will changes within the same person and from person to person. Even if human wills were to come to an agreement on some common ground, according to a shared ethical foundation, this would be minimal in its contents, uncertain in its application, and weak in its effects.

- In the reality and laws of the state. "Entrusting exclusively to individual states, with their laws and institutions, the final responsibility to meet the aspirations of persons, communities and entire peoples, can sometimes have consequences that exclude the possibility of a social order respectful of the dignity and rights of the person" (Pope Benedict XVI, Address to the General Assembly of the United Nations).

- In the legal system. "When presented purely in terms of legality, rights risk becoming weak propositions divorced from the ethical and rational dimension which is their foundation and their goal" (op. cit.).

✠ The ultimate source of human rights lies in the transcendent dignity of the human person as created in the image of God, and therefore, in the final analysis, in God the Creator. If this solid ethical basis is ignored, human rights remain fragile, because they do not have a strong foundation.

In fact, having been created in the image of God, human beings are

- The highest point of God's plan for the world and for history, the summit of the visible creation
- "The only creatures on earth that God has willed for their own sake and has called to share, through knowledge and love, in his own divine life . . . A person is not something but someone, capable of self-knowledge and of freely giving himself and entering into communion with God and with other persons" (*Compendium of the CCC*, no. 66).
- The subject, foundation, and objective of these rights
- At the heart of the institutions, laws, and initiatives of society

✠ "Strictly speaking, these human rights are not truths of faith, even though they are discoverable—and indeed come to full light—in the message of Christ who 'reveals man to man himself' (*Gaudium et Spes*, no. 22). They receive further confirmation from faith. Yet it stands to reason that, living and acting in the physical world as spiritual beings, men and women ascertain the pervading presence of a logos which enables them to distinguish not only between true and false, but also good and evil, better and worse, and justice and injustice" (Pope Benedict XVI, Address to the Pontifical Academy of Social Sciences, May 4, 2009).

✠ "[These rights] are based on the natural law inscribed on human hearts and present in different cultures and civilizations. Removing human rights from this context would mean restricting their range and yielding to a relativistic conception, according to which the meaning and interpretation of rights could vary and their universality would be denied in the name of different cultural, political, social and even religious outlooks" (Pope Benedict XVI, Address to the General Assembly of the United Nations).

What is the natural law?

"The natural law which is inscribed by the Creator on the heart of every person consists in a participation in the wisdom and the goodness of God. It expresses that original moral sense which enables one to discern by reason the good and the bad. It is universal and immutable and determines the basis of the duties and fundamental rights of the person as well as those of the human community and civil law" (*Compendium of the* CCC, no. 416).

"The natural law 'is nothing other than the light of intellect infused within us by God. Thanks to this, we know what must be done and what must be avoided. This light or this law has been given by God to creation' (St. Thomas Aquinas, *In Duo Praecepta Caritatis et in Decem Legis Praecepta Expositio*, ch 1). It consists in the participation in his eternal law, which is identified with God himself (cf. St. Thomas Aquinas, *Summa Theologiae*, I-II, q. 91, a. 2, c). This law is called 'natural' because the reason that promulgates it is proper to human nature. It is universal, it extends to all people insofar as it is established by reason. In its principal precepts, the divine and natural law is presented in the Decalogue and indicates the primary and essential norms regulating moral life (cf. CCC, 1955). Its central focus is the act of aspiring and submitting to God, the source and judge of everything that is good, and also the act of seeing others as equal to oneself. The natural law expresses the dignity of the person and lays the foundations of the person's fundamental duties" (*Compendium of the Social Doctrine of the Church*, no. 140).

The natural law is nothing other than a participation in the eternal law: "*Unde . . . lex universalis nihil aliud est quam participatio legis aeternae in rationali creatura*" (St. Thomas Aquinas, *Summa Theologiae*, I-II, 91, 2).

What are the characteristics of human rights?

These rights are

✠ "*Universal*, because they are present in all human beings, without exception of time, place or subject

✠ "*Inviolable*, insofar as 'they are inherent in the human person and in human dignity' (Pope John Paul II, Message for the 1999 World Day of Peace, 3: AAS 91 (1999), p. 379) and because 'it would be vain to proclaim rights, if at the same time everything were not done to ensure the duty of respecting them by all people, everywhere, and for all people' (Pope Paul VI, Message to the International Conference on Human Rights, Tehran (April 15, 1968): *L'Osservatore Romano*, English edition, May 2, 1968, p. 4]

✠ "*Inalienable*, insofar as 'no one can legitimately deprive another person, whoever they may be, of these rights, since this would do violence to their nature'" (*Compendium of the Social Doctrine of the Church*, no. 153, emphasis added)

✠ *Indivisible*: They form a whole, like a single right, standing or falling together; each one reflects the others, each is complementary and irreplaceable. "Together they form a single whole, directed unambiguously towards the promotion of every aspect of the good of both the person and society . . . The integral promotion of every category of human rights is the true guarantee of full respect for each individual right" (Pope John Paul II, Message for the World Day for Peace, 1999, no. 3).

Are human rights connected to justice?

Of course. "Since rights and the resulting duties follow naturally from human interaction, it is easy to forget that they are the fruit of a commonly held sense of justice built primarily upon solidarity among the members of society, and hence valid at all times and for all peoples. This intuition was expressed as early as the fifth century by Augustine of Hippo, one of the masters of our intellectual heritage. He taught that the saying: Do not do to others what you would not want done to you 'cannot in any way vary according to the different understandings that have arisen in the world' (*De Doctrina Christiana*, III, 14). Human rights, then, must be respected as an expression of justice, and not merely because they are enforceable through the will of the legislators" (Pope Benedict XVI, Address to the General Assembly of the United Nations).

What is the relationship between rights and duties?

✠ There is a profound correlation, a mutual complementarity, a correlative responsibility between rights and duties.

Rights and duties are indissolubly conjoined, first of all in the human person to whom they belong. This bond also presents a social dimension: "In human society one man's natural right gives rise to a corresponding duty in other men; the duty, that is, of recognizing and respecting that right. . . . Hence, to claim one's rights and ignore one's duties, or only half fulfill them, is like building a house with one hand and tearing it down with the other" (Blessed John XXIII, *Pacem in Terris*, no. 30).

✠ It is therefore necessary

- To insist adequately on the duties that stem from the corresponding rights. In reality, duties that establish rights must be limited so that they do not become arbitrary. The limitation on rights comes from duties. "The Ganges of rights flows from the Himalaya of duties," Gandhi said.
- To move from an age that tends to emphasize rights to a new phase of history in which duties are also given just consideration
- To avoid disguising egotistical and subjective demands as rights, or artificially inventing a duty as the justification for a new right. This would create a Babel of rights, which would lead to an almost exclusive prevalence of the right of the strongest.

Do nations have rights?

"The rights of nations are nothing but 'human rights fostered at the specific level of community life.' A nation has a 'fundamental right to existence,' to 'its own language and culture, through which a people expresses and promotes . . . its fundamental spiritual sovereignty,' to 'shape its life according to its own traditions, excluding, of course, every abuse of basic human rights and in particular the oppression of minorities,' to 'build its future by providing an appropriate education for the younger generation.' The international order requires a balance between particularity and universality, which all nations are called to bring about, for their primary duty is to live in a posture of peace, respect and solidarity with other nations" (*Compendium of the Social Doctrine of the Church*, no. 157).

Is there a gap between letter and spirit in human rights?

Unfortunately, there is a gap between letter and spirit in human rights, which are often paid nothing but ceremonial respect. In fact, there is a glaring contradiction between the solemn proclamation of human rights and their implementation, their practical application. Anyone can see that there exists a painful reality of violations of every kind and in a great number of places.

Who is responsible for defending and promoting these rights?

"Every state has the primary duty to protect its own population from grave and sustained violations of human rights, as well as from the consequences of humanitarian crises, whether natural or man-made. If states are unable to guarantee such protection, the international community must intervene with the juridical means provided in the United Nations Charter and in other international instruments. The action of the international community and its institutions, provided that it respects the principles undergirding the international order, should never be interpreted as an unwarranted imposition or a limitation of sovereignty. On the contrary, it is indifference or failure to intervene that do the real damage . . . The promotion of human rights remains the most effective strategy for eliminating inequalities between countries and social groups, and for increasing security" (Pope Benedict XVI, Address to the General Assembly of the United Nations).

What is the task of the Church with regard to human rights?

✠ In its mission, which is and remains essentially religious in nature, the Church

- Includes the defense and promotion of fundamental human rights
- "Greatly esteems the dynamic movements of today by which these rights are everywhere fostered" (*Gaudium et Spes*, no. 41)
- Strives to respect justice and human rights within the Church itself
- Proclaims the Christian foundation of human rights

- Denounces violations of these rights
- Trusts above all in the help of the Lord and of his Spirit in promoting these rights
- Is open to collaboration with all religions, with people of every race and culture, with all organizations—governmental and nongovernmental, national and international—that are working to promote and defend these rights

✠ "Promoting justice and peace, penetrating with the light and leaven of the Gospel all areas of social existence, has always been a constant commitment of the Church in the name of the mandate that it has received from the Lord" (Pope Paul VI, *Iustitiam et Pacem*).

✠ Although "we have undoubtedly come a long way already," "there is still a long way to go; hundreds of millions of our brothers and sisters still see their rights to life, to freedom and to security threatened. Neither the equality of all nor the dignity of each person is always respected, while new barriers are raised for reasons linked to race, religion, political opinion or other convictions" (Pope Benedict XVI, Address, December 10, 2008).

For more on this topic, see the following pontifical documents:

Blessed John XXIII, *Pacem in Terris*, 1963
Paul VI, Address to the General Assembly of the United Nations, October 4, 1965; Message to the

International Conference on Human Rights, April 15, 1968; *Octogesima Adveniens*, 1971

Vatican Council II, *Gaudium et Spes*, *Dignitatis Humanae*

John Paul II, Address to the 34th General Assembly of the United Nations, October 2, 1979; Address to the Fiftieth General Assembly of the United Nations, October 5, 1995; *Sollicitudo Rei Socialis*, 1988; *Centesimus Annus*, 1991; *Veritatis Splendor*, 1993; *Evangelium Vitae*, 1995

Catechism of the Catholic Church, nos. 337-361, 2104-2109

Compendium of the CCC, nos. 62-68, 444

Pontifical Council for Justice and Peace, *Compendium of the Social Doctrine of the Church*, 2004

Benedict XVI, Address to the General Assembly of the United Nations, April 18, 2008

III
Human Embryo

What is the embryo?

The embryo is the fruit of the fusion of two germ cells, one from the mother (oocyte) and the other from the father (spermatozoon). This process of fusion is called fertilization or conception, which gives rise to the life cycle of a human individual.

What dignity does the embryo enjoy?

It enjoys the dignity of a human being and therefore its right to life from its first days of intense and autonomous activity according to the law written in the program plan inscribed in its DNA.

What does science say about the human embryo?

✠ Some data of a scientific, medical, genetic nature illustrate the identity of the human embryo starting from conception. Scientific research has demonstrated how the embryo possesses its own individual identity from conception: it is a human being in progress. It is through fertilization that individual—and therefore personal—life begins for each one of us. This is documented by countless studies of cell biology and cytogenetics, molecular genetics, the biology of reproduction and development, and obstetrics.

✠ Knowledge of the biological truth of the human embryo and rational reflection on its real ontological status therefore lead to the affirmation that the human embryo is not something, but someone. In fact:

- From the biological point of view, human formation and development appear as a unique, continuous, coordinated, and gradual process beginning at fertilization, with which a new human organism is constituted that is endowed with an intrinsic capacity to develop autonomously into an adult individual. The most recent contributions of the biomedical sciences have provided valuable experimental evidence for the concept of the individuality and continuity of embryonic development.
- From the moment in which the egg is fertilized, a new life is begun that is not that of the father or mother, but of a new human being that develops for its own sake. It will never be made human if it has not been so since then. This doctrine remains valid and is therefore confirmed, if there were need, by the recent achievements of human biology, which recognizes that in the zygote derived from the fertilization

of the two gametes there is already found the biological identity of a new human individual.

■ By virtue of conception itself, at that very moment the human being is endowed not only with a genetic condition, but also with a unique anthropological value and with fundamental rights to life, health, and physical integrity.

■ The techniques of artificial fertilization themselves—by bringing about conception under microscopic observation in a laboratory—document with inexorable evidence that what is implanted and will grow in the mother's womb, the embryo, has already been formed and begun to develop from the moment of fertilization. What takes place in the laboratory is the same process that happens naturally in the mother's womb.

Paradoxically, the proponents of artificial fertilization and experimentation on the human embryo who want to justify its manipulation and destruction by denying its identity as a human being are precisely the ones who have demonstrated through their scientific research and clinical practices that the human embryo is one of us, because each of us was like it at the beginning of our lives. The reasonableness of this affirmation lies in the (unquestionable) fact that if our existence had been interrupted when we were an embryo, we would never have seen the light of day.

■ The fertilized oocyte is a human being from the first phases of its development, operates as an individual distinct from the mother, and is intrinsically oriented to a precise individual evolution. All of this requires the absolute defense of the embryo, against any intervention that would block the progress of the pregnancy.

✠ What is at work here is not faith, but reason, and therefore the response applies to all, believers and nonbelievers.

So what are the characteristics of the embryo according to science?

✠ The embryo is already an individual, operates as an individual distinct from the mother, with a precise somatic individuality. That is, we are in the presence of a biological entity that has its own precise "individuality" in its body (soma): the embryo displays its own individuality, which is fully accessible to the analysis of the cytogeneticist who observes it. Now, today, we are very attentive to our "somatic individuality," meaning our bodily identity. We no longer say, "I have a body," but, "I am my body."

✠ The embryo presents itself as absolutely unique and unrepeatable. That is, every human embryo is "unique." There has never been and never will be another identical to it. Now, this is precisely what anthropologically we refer to as human dignity: every human being is unique, every human being can give to the world that which no other can ever give it, every human being, because of his or her unrepeatability, is worthy of the love of others because they can receive from him or her what no other can ever give them. It is a mistake to say that the embryo is "undifferentiated" in its first days of life, because if placed in different environments it could become many things other than a human being. It is like saying a living man is undifferentiated because if we put him in fire he would become ash, or if we put him in the ground he would become dust.

✠ The embryo is a human being in development according to a plan already fixed from conception. This development is to be understood not in the sense of an ontological, qualitative transformation, but in the sense of a homogenous evolution, of harmonious development. The human being has an active and intrinsic capacity for development, and not a mere possibility of life. That is, everything that the embryo is from that moment on, its whole biological history, is already present in code. Everything that will take shape is already present in the genome of the embryo, from the first moment. For this reason, it can never be accepted that the embryo is a human being "in potentiality," because the embryo already is all that it is: only its development is in potentiality. That is, we have before us, not a human being in potentiality but not yet in reality, but a human being who already has within himself or herself all the future potentialities of development.

✠ The embryo is a *terminus a quo* already destined by nature to translate itself into the *terminus ad quem* of its intrinsic dynamism; and not into just any sort of *terminus ad quem*, but only into that which corresponds to the ontological indications of its nature.

✠ The embryo is a being different from an adult, but these differences must be seen within a conception of human life that recognizes different stages, from childhood to old age.

✠ The embryo, even from a strictly biological point of view, is not simply a passive receptor, but interacts with its vital environment.

✠ The embryo is the bearer of an anthropological dignity. By virtue of the substantial unity of the body with the spirit, the embryo does not have only a biological meaning. It is the bearer of an anthropological dignity, which has its foundation in the spiritual soul that pervades and enlivens it.

✠ The embryo is a human being who is a child from the very first stages of his or her existence, meaning from the moment in which the genetic makeup of the father and mother are united. All of this marks and influences the embryo's membership in the human species, the hereditary bond and the biological and somatic notes of individuality. Its influence on the structure of the physical being is decisive from the dawn of conception until natural death.

✠ The embryo is the weakest of all human creatures.

Is the embryo a person?

Science cannot say anything in this regard, since the concept of personhood is beyond the competence of science. Even the

Church does not say explicitly that the embryo is a person. Nonetheless, it must be reaffirmed that this value of personhood is not bestowed on the human subject by parents, society, or the state, or by reaching a certain age. On the contrary, being a person is a connatural prerogative of the human being. The "concept," the "value" of personhood accompanies the individual from conception to natural death. It is always present, even when the person does not have the faculty of intending and willing: in the mother's womb, while sleeping, in a coma.

The Catholic Church certainly does not rule out a priori that the embryo is a person, but it does not affirm it definitively. The instruction *Donum Vitae* of the Congregation for the Doctrine of the Faith (CDF) refers to "respect for the human being from the first moment of his or her existence" (Foreword).

"The reality of the human being for the entire span of life, both before and after birth, does not allow us to posit either a change in nature or a gradation in moral value, since it possesses *full anthropological and ethical status*. The human embryo has, therefore, from the very beginning, the dignity proper to a person" (CDF, *Dignitas Personae*, no. 5).

What does the Christian faith say about the embryo?

✠ The Christian faith accepts the scientific conception described above.

Conclusions of a scientific nature are accepted by the Magisterium of the Church not as incontrovertible proof but as a valuable indication for rationally discerning a human presence from the first appearance of a human life. The theological perspective, beginning with the light that revelation sheds on the meaning of human life and on the dignity of the person, reinforces and supports human reason in its scientific collisions, without prejudging the validity of the achievements gained through rational evidence.

✠ The Christian faith goes beyond—it completes—the aforementioned scientific achievements. In fact, it affirms that

- From the mother's womb, the person belongs to God, who examines and knows all, who forms and shapes it with his hands, who sees it while it is still a tiny formless embryo, and sees in it the adult of tomorrow, whose days are numbered and whose vocation is already written in the "book of life" (see Ps 139:1, 13-16). Even when still in the mother's womb—as attested to by many biblical passages (see Jer 1:4-5; Ps 71:6; Is 46:3; Job 10:8-12; Ps 22:10-11, as well as the texts from Luke)—the human being is the exquisitely personal end of the fatherly providence of God.
- The human being has the dignity of a creature that God has willed for its own sake
- The human embryo, as a human being, is in a special relationship with God. The embryo is related thus not only to those from whom the original components that constitute it come (its parents), but also to the ultimate source of all life, which the Christian recognizes as God.

✠ The uniqueness and unrepeatability of the embryo also has a theological value. Just as God in his most profound identity is absolutely unique and unrepeatable, so also he has so loved the human being as to inscribe his image in our flesh, in our genetic structure.

✠ Moreover, what happens in human fertilization is the generation of a human being. The parents are not vegetable or animal. So from the beginning, the embryo is designed by nature to receive a spiritual soul from God.

✠ The fact that the embryo has its own somatic individuality also has theological value. God has so loved our bodiliness as to choose to become incarnate in his Son Jesus Christ, to make himself body like us, so that we may know him.

What are the effects of this special relationship that God has with the embryo?

✠ In giving life to the embryo, God creates it in his image and likeness.

✠ In what sense is the human being created "in the image of God"?

- "The human person is created in the image of God in the sense that he or she is capable of knowing and of loving their Creator in freedom. Human beings are the only creatures on earth that God has willed for their own sake and has called to share, through knowledge and love, in his own divine life. All human beings, in as much as they are created in the image of God, have the dignity of a person. A person is not something but someone, capable of self-knowledge and of freely giving himself and entering into communion with God and with other persons" (*Compendium of the CCC*, no. 66).

✠ "God himself, in creating man in his own image, has written upon his heart the desire to see him. Even if this desire is often ignored, God never ceases to draw man to himself because only in God will he find and live the fullness of truth and happiness for which he never stops searching. By nature and by vocation, therefore, man is a religious being, capable of entering into communion with God. This intimate and vital bond with God confers on man his fundamental dignity" (*Compendium of the CCC*, no. 2).

✠ God gives the human embryo a spiritual soul, which does not come from the parents but is created directly by God and is immortal.

✠ The fruit of human generation, from the first moment of its existence, demands the unconditional respect that is morally due to the human being in his or her physical and spiritual totality.

✠ Physical human life is a primary and fundamental good, which demands to be promoted, defended, and respected, while still waiting for the fulfillment of its perfection that will be realized in its supernatural and eternal condition.

✠ The recognition of life as a gift created by God orients the human person toward living life as a gift to be donated to his or her Creator and brothers and sisters.

✠ Parents—not excluding the *paterfamilias*—do not have absolute power over their children. The life of the unborn child is under the dominion of God, the only one who can give it and can take it away.

From where does the duty to respect the embryo come?

✠ The ethical attitude of respect and care for life, for the dignity and integrity of the embryo, is

- Demanded by the presence of a human being who must be considered a person
- Motivated by a unified conception of the person (*corpore et anima unus*) that must be recognized from the first moment of life
- Justified by the fact that no human being can ever be reduced to a means but is always an end
- Motivated by the fact that the embryo is a human being and therefore sacred, being a human life. Human life, an inalienable and inviolable good, is sacred because, from its beginning, it involves "the creative action of God" and remains forever in a special relationship with the Creator, its sole end. The

unborn child is someone whose dignity must always be honored and defended in all the phases of its growth and development, until the attainment of the fullness of the adult condition.

✠ The duty to respect the human embryo as a human person therefore stems from the reality of things and the power of rational argumentation, and not exclusively from a position of faith.

✠ It must also be emphasized that the Church's position is not an imposition made in the name of the faith that it professes, thereby acting—as some attempt to believe—to impede scientific progress, but on the contrary, as expressly affirmed in the instruction *Donum Vitae* of the CDF, a contribution "inspired also by the love which she owes to man, helping him to recognize and respect his rights and duties."

This recognition is dictated by reason, meaning that it is reached by the person who reflects on themselves and on their actions, deriving their responsibilities from this.

What must be rejected for the sake of protecting the embryo?

✠ The idea must be rejected that the human embryo is

- A "lump of tissue" that does not constitute a real human individual, but only a "potentiality" to become such at a given moment (to be established by convention) in the process of its development

- A valuable technological tool under the banner of "good medical practice," on the pretext of scientific, technological, and specifically medical progress, in view of important new therapeutic avenues in service of humanity. This leads to the exploitation of the embryo, an exploitation that is all the more deplorable in that it is often pursued for financial purposes.
- Mere "biological material," without its own identity in the scheme of life and without the dignity proper to the human being, which can therefore be treated as an "object"
- Unworthy of any special moral attention, nor of a special status as a potential human being, but rather a respect that is proportional to its level of development, a respect counterbalanced, above all in the initial phases, by the potential benefits to be gained from research

✠ The following must be rejected:

- Any intervention on the genome that is not intended for the good of the person, understood as a unity of body and spirit, or that would violate its integrity and dignity
- Any kind of manipulation that would put the life of the embryo in grave danger, such as analysis, cryopreservation ("freezing") as an alternative to transfer in utero, scientific experiments on the embryo, in

particular when it is outside the mother's body ("test tube"), or the selection of embryos through genetic diagnosis prior to their implantation in utero

■ The voluntary destruction of the embryo, which is an abortion, a homicide. And it must be noted that "the freedom to kill is not true freedom, but a tyranny that reduces the human being to slavery" (Pope Benedict XVI, Homily, May 7, 2005).

What is the Church's view of the destruction of the embryo?

The Church has always considered the deliberate destruction of the unborn child a particularly cruel offense. "What is at stake is so important that, from the standpoint of moral obligation, the mere probability that a human person is involved would suffice to justify an absolutely clear prohibition of any intervention aimed at killing a human embryo . . . 'The human being is to be respected and treated as a person from the moment of conception'" (*Evangelium Vitae*, no. 60).

What does the Catholic Church think about the embryo resulting from artificial fertilization?

The embryo, even if it has been conceived through artificial fertilization (not morally acceptable), has all the rights and duties of any other person, has the same dignity, and deserves the same respect as any other human being.

What is the duty of the state?

✠ States and positive laws have the task of recognizing, not creating, a definition of the human being, in that it is not authority but truth that constitutes rights. And the truth is that from the moment of fertilization there begins a continual process of the development of a new individual, which cannot be arbitrarily divided into phases with different values, and therefore with a different degree of protection, and that its genetic makeup is that of the adult individual that will develop.

It is not the place of positive law to define the ontology of the human being.

✠ From the legal point of view, the central point of the debate over the protection of the human embryo is not whether it is possible to identify thresholds of humanity more or less delayed with respect to fertilization, but concerns the recognition of fundamental human rights by reason of being a person, and demands above all, in the name of the principle of equality, the right to life and to physical integrity from the first moment of existence. The unborn child has rights that must also be protected by human legislation, all the more so in that the unborn child belongs to the category of the weak and defenseless. For example, the unborn child has the right to have a mother and father and to know who they are; the right to a biological, societal, and affective identity.

Is the Church opposed to scientific research?

✠ Certainly not, and history demonstrates this. The Church is opposed to a certain kind of research on the part of science, such as that which would lower the embryo to the level of a laboratory instrument. Scientific research in the field of genetics must be encouraged and promoted, but like every other human activity, it can never be devoid of moral imperatives.

✠ The good and authentic achievements of science reveal the Creator's greatness ever more, because they allow human beings to realize the order inherent in creation and to appreciate the wonders of their bodies as well as that of their intellects, in which is reflected, to some extent, the light of the Word through whom "all things came to be" (Jn 1:3).

✠ Science, and in particular the scientist, must respect the moral norms. For example:

- Not everything that is scientifically and technologically feasible is also morally acceptable.
- It is not right to obtain good through evil.
- The ends do not justify the means. Therefore service of life must be realized through licit means.
- As for life (whether in birth, life, or death), we are neither masters nor creators, but administrators.
- The sacred context of life must be protected (above all in birth and death).

✠ John Paul II left the members of the Pontifical Academy for Sciences with an incisive reminder on October 28, 1994: "We must not allow ourselves to be dazzled by the myth of progress, as if the possibility of carrying out research or implementing a technology allowed us to classify them immediately as morally good. The moral goodness is measured by the authentic good that is obtained for the human person considered according to the twofold physical and spiritual dimension."

For more on this topic, see the following pontifical documents:

Catechism of the Catholic Church, nos. 355-384; 2258-2330
Compendium of the CCC, nos. 2-5; 466-486; 499-501
Congregation for the Doctrine of the Faith, Donum Vitae, no. 198

IV
Dignity of the Human Person

Contemporary Bioethics Questions

This section presents a summary of some important points of the instruction *Dignitas Personae: On Certain Bioethical Questions* (DP), published on September 8, 2008, by the CDF. This instruction was expressly approved by the Holy Father Benedict XVI. It therefore belongs to those documents which "participate in the ordinary magisterium of the successor of Peter" (instruction *Donum Veritatis*, no. 18), to be welcomed by the faithful with "the religious assent of their spirit" (DP, no. 37).

Why this document?

✠ In recent years, the biomedical sciences have made enormous progress, which opens new therapeutic perspectives but also raises serious questions.

✠ The aforementioned instruction seeks to

- Present answers to some new questions of bioethics, which provoke uncertainty and perplexity in vast sectors of society
- "[Contribute] to the formation of conscience" and encourage biomedical research respectful of the dignity of every human being and of procreation, giving a voice to those who have none, to those who are totally defenseless, as the human embryo certainly is

✠ In proceeding with the examination of these new questions, "the Congregation for the Doctrine of the Faith has benefited from the analysis of the Pontifical Academy for Life and has consulted numerous experts with regard to the scientific aspects of these questions, in order to address them with the principles of Christian anthropology. The encyclicals *Veritatis Splendor* and *Evangelium Vitae* of John Paul II, as well as other interventions of the magisterium, offer clear indications with regard to both the method and the content of the examination of the problems under consideration" (DP, no. 2).

✠ In proposing moral principles and assessments for biomedical research on human life, the Church "draws upon *the light both of reason and of faith* and seeks to set forth an integral vision of man and his vocation, capable of incorporating everything that is good in human activity, as well as in various cultural and religious traditions which not infrequently demonstrate a great reverence for life" (DP, no. 3).

On what fundamental principle is the instruction based?

✠ It is based on the dignity of the person, which must be recognized in every human being, from conception to natural death. This fundamental principle "expresses *a great 'yes' to human life* and must be at the center of ethical reflection on biomedical research" (DP, no. 1).

✠ In particular:

- "The human being is to be respected and treated as a person from the moment of conception; and therefore from that same moment his rights as a person must be recognized, among which in the first place is the inviolable right of every innocent human being to life" (DP, no. 4).
- "It is the Church's conviction that what is human is not only received and respected by faith, but is also purified, elevated and perfected" (DP, no. 7). God has created every human being in his image. In his Incarnate Son, he has fully revealed the mystery of humanity. The Son makes it possible for us to become children of God. "By taking the interrelationship of these two dimensions, the human and the divine, as the starting point, one understands better why it is that man has unassailable value: he possesses an eternal vocation and is called to share in the trinitarian love of the living God" (DP, no. 8).
- "*The origin of human life has its authentic context in marriage and in the family*, where it is generated through an act which expresses the reciprocal love between a

man and a woman. Procreation which is truly responsible vis-à-vis the child to be born 'must be the fruit
of marriage'" (DP, no. 6).

■ "These two dimensions of life, the natural and the
supernatural, allow us to understand better the sense
in which the acts that permit a new human being to
come into existence, in which a man and a woman
give themselves to each other, are a reflection of trinitarian love. 'God, who is love and life, has inscribed in
man and woman the vocation to share in a special way
in his mystery of personal communion and in his work
as Creator and Father' . . . 'The Holy Spirit who is
poured out in the sacramental celebration offers Christian couples the gift of a new communion of love that
is the living and real image of that unique unity which
makes of the Church the indivisible Mystical Body of
the Lord Jesus" (DP, no. 9).

It must be reiterated:

■ Man will always be greater than all the elements
that form his body; indeed, he carries within him the
power of thought which always aspires to the truth
about himself and about the world.

■ Every human being, therefore, is far more than a
unique combination of genetic information that is
transmitted by his or her parents.

■ Human generation can never be reduced to the mere
reproduction of a new individual of the human species, as happens with any animal. (Pope Benedict

XVI, Address to the members of the Pontifical Academy for Life, February 21, 2009)

✠ Therefore, saying "yes" to the dignity of the human being necessarily entails saying "no" to anything that goes against respect for this dignity. The "nos" that the Church says are therefore the flip side of a positive vision, of "yeses" that the Church proclaims on behalf of the truth and dignity of the person.

What is the relationship between the ecclesiastical Magisterium and the autonomy of the sciences?

"The Church, by expressing an ethical judgment on some developments of recent medical research concerning man and his beginnings, does not intervene in the area proper to medical science itself, but rather calls everyone to ethical and social responsibility for their actions. She reminds them that the ethical value of biomedical science is gauged in reference to both the unconditional respect owed to every human being at every moment of his or her existence, and the defense of the specific character of the personal act which transmits life" (DP, no. 10).

What does the Church say about the techniques for assisting human fertility?

✠ About the techniques aimed at overcoming infertility, such as

- "Techniques of heterologous artificial fertilization" (DP, no. 12), "used to obtain a human conception artificially by the use of gametes coming from at least one donor other than the spouses who are joined in marriage" (DP, footnote 22)

- "Techniques of homologous artificial fertilization" (DP, no. 12), "used to obtain a human conception using the gametes of the two spouses joined in marriage" (DP, footnote 23)
- "Techniques which act *as an aid to the conjugal act and its fertility*" (DP, no. 12)
- "Techniques aimed at removing obstacles to natural fertilization" (DP, no. 13)
- Adoption (DP, no. 13)

the Church affirms that all techniques are licit that respect

- The right to life and to physical integrity of every human being from conception to natural death
- The unity of marriage, which means reciprocal respect for the right within marriage to become a father or mother only together with the other spouse
- The specifically human values of sexuality which require "that the procreation of a human person be brought about as the fruit of the conjugal act specific to the love between spouses" (DP, no. 12)

✠ Therefore, "techniques which assist procreation 'are not to be rejected on the grounds that they are artificial' . . . techniques which act as an aid to the conjugal act and its fertility are permitted . . . 'A medical intervention respects the dignity of persons when it seeks to assist the conjugal act either in order to facilitate its performance or in order to enable it to achieve its objective once it has been normally performed'" (DP, no. 12).

✠ "Certainly, techniques aimed at removing obstacles to natural fertilization, as for example, hormonal treatments for infertility, surgery for endometriosis, unblocking of fallopian tubes or their surgical repair, are licit" (DP, no. 13).

✠ "Adoption should be encouraged, promoted and facilitated by appropriate legislation so that the many children who lack parents may receive a home that will contribute to their human development. In addition, research and investment directed at the prevention of sterility deserve encouragement" (DP, no. 13).

What is to be said of in vitro fertilization?

✠ The experience of recent years has demonstrated that in the context of in vitro fertilization, "*the number of embryos sacrificed is extremely high*" (DP, no. 14). "Currently the number of embryos sacrificed, even in the most technically advanced centers of artificial fertilization, hovers above 80%" (see DP, footnote 27).

- "Embryos produced in vitro which have defects are directly discarded.
- "Cases are becoming ever more prevalent in which couples who have no fertility problems are using artificial means of procreation in order to engage in genetic selection of their offspring."

- Among the embryos produced in vitro, "some are transferred into the woman's uterus, while the others are frozen for future use."

- The technique of multiple transfer, by which "the number of embryos transferred is greater than the single child desired, in the expectation that some embryos will be lost . . . implies a *purely utilitarian treatment of embryos*" (DP, no. 15).

✠ "The blithe acceptance of the enormous number of abortions involved in the process of in vitro fertilization vividly illustrates how the replacement of the conjugal act by a technical procedure . . . leads to a weakening of the respect owed to every human being. Recognition of such respect is, on the other hand, promoted by the intimacy of husband and wife nourished by married love . . . In the face of this manipulation of the human being in his or her embryonic state, it needs to be repeated that God's love does not differentiate between the newly conceived infant still in his or her mother's womb and the child or young person, or the adult and the elderly person. God does not distinguish between them because he sees an impression of his own image and likeness (Gn 1:26) in each one . . . Therefore, the magisterium of the Church has constantly proclaimed the sacred and inviolable character of every human life from its conception until its natural end" (DP, no. 16).

What is to be said about the freezing of oocytes?

"In order to avoid the serious ethical problems posed by the freezing of embryos, the freezing of oocytes has also been advanced in the area of techniques of in vitro fertilization" (DP, no. 20).

In this regard, the cryopreservation of oocytes, although not immoral in itself and considered in other contexts that are not examined here, *"for the purpose of being used in artificial procreation is to be considered morally unacceptable"* (DP, no. 20).

Embryo reduction?

"Some techniques used in artificial procreation, above all the transfer of multiple embryos into the mother's womb, have caused a significant increase in the frequency of multiple pregnancy. This situation gives rise in turn to the practice of so-called embryo reduction, a procedure in which embryos or fetuses in the womb are directly exterminated . . . From the ethical point of view, *embryo reduction is an intentional selective abortion*. It is in fact the deliberate and direct elimination of one or more innocent human beings in the initial phase of their existence and as such it always constitutes a grave moral disorder" (DP, no. 12).

Preimplantation diagnosis?

"Preimplantation diagnosis is a form of prenatal diagnosis connected with techniques of artificial fertilization in which embryos formed in vitro undergo genetic diagnosis before being transferred into a woman's womb. Such diagnosis is done *in order to ensure that only embryos free from defects or having the desired sex or other particular qualities are transferred"* (DP, no. 22).

"Unlike other forms of prenatal diagnosis . . . the diagnosis before implantation is immediately followed by the elimination of an embryo suspected of having genetic or chromosomal defects, or not having the sex desired, or having other qualities that are not wanted. Preimplantation diagnosis . . . is directed toward the qualitative selection and consequent destruction of embryos, which constitutes an act of abortion . . . By treating the human embryo as mere 'laboratory material,' the concept itself of human dignity is also subjected to alteration and discrimination . . . Such discrimination is immoral and must therefore be considered legally unacceptable" (DP, no. 22).

New forms of interception and contragestation

"Such methods are *interceptive* if they interfere with the embryo before implantation" (DP, no. 23), for example through "the IUD (intrauterine device) and the so-called 'morning-after pills'" (DP, footnote 43). They are "contragestative if they cause the elimination of the embryo once implanted" (DP, no. 23), for example through "RU-486 (Mifepristone), synthetic prostaglandins or Methotrexate" (DP, footnote 44).

✠ Although interceptives do not cause an abortion every time they are used, in part because fertilization does not always take place immediately after sexual relations, it must be noted "that anyone who seeks to prevent the implantation of an embryo which may possibly have been conceived and who therefore either requests or prescribes such a pharmaceutical, generally intends abortion." In the case of contragestation, "what takes place in reality is the *abortion of an embryo which has just implanted* . . . The use of means of interception and contragestation fall within the *sin of abortion* and are gravely immoral" (DP, no. 23).

What is the Church's view on gene therapy?

✠ By gene therapy is meant "techniques of genetic engineering applied to human beings for therapeutic purposes, that is to say, with the aim of curing genetically based diseases." Somatic gene therapy, for its part, "seeks to eliminate or reduce genetic defects on the level of somatic cells." Germ line cell therapy "aims instead at correcting genetic defects present in germ line cells with the purpose of transmitting the therapeutic effects to the offspring of the individual" (DP, no. 25).

✠ From the ethical point of view, the following applies:

- As for somatic gene therapy, these "*are in principle morally licit* . . . Given that gene therapy can involve significant risks for the patient, the ethical principle must be observed according to which, in order to proceed to a therapeutic intervention, it is necessary to establish beforehand that the person being treated will not be exposed to risks to his health or physical integrity which are excessive or disproportionate to the gravity of the pathology for which a cure is sought. The informed consent of the patient or his legitimate representative is also required" (DP, no. 26).
- As for germ line cell therapy, "because the risks connected to any genetic manipulation are considerable

and as yet not fully controllable, *in the present state of research, it is not morally permissible to act in a way that may cause possible harm to the resulting progeny*" (DP, no. 26).

■ As for the hypothesis of applying genetic engineering for the presumed aims of improving and strengthening the gene pool, it must be observed that such manipulations would foster "a eugenic mentality" and would introduce "indirect social stigma with regard to people who lack certain qualities, while privileging qualities that happen to be appreciated by a certain culture or society; such qualities do not constitute what is specifically human. This would be in contrast with the fundamental truth of the equality of all human beings which is expressed in the principle of justice, the violation of which, in the long run, would harm peaceful coexistence among individuals . . . Finally it must also be noted that in the attempt to create a new type of human being one can recognize an ideological element in which man tries to take the place of his Creator" (DP, no. 27).

Is human cloning morally acceptable?

✠ By human cloning is meant "the asexual or agametic reproduction of the entire human organism in order to produce one or more 'copies' which, from a genetic perspective, are substantially identical to the single original" (DP, no. 28). The techniques proposed for human cloning are embryo splitting, which consists in "the artificial separation of individual cells or groups of cells from the embryo in the earliest stage of development. These are then transferred into the uterus in order to obtain identical embryos in an artificial manner" (DP, footnote 47), and nuclear transfer, which consists in "introducing a nucleus taken from an embryonic or somatic cell into a denucleated oocyte. This is followed by stimulation of the oocyte so that it begins to develop as an embryo" (DP, footnote 47). Cloning is proposed for two reasons: reproductive (or to obtain the birth of a cloned child) and for therapeutic or research purposes.

✠ Cloning is "intrinsically illicit in that, by taking the ethical negativity of techniques of artificial fertilization to their extreme, it seeks to give rise to a new human being without a connection to the act of reciprocal self-giving between the spouses and, more radically, without any link to sexuality. This leads to manipulation and abuses gravely injurious to human dignity" (DP, no. 28).

   ▪ As for reproductive cloning, this "would impose on the resulting individual a predetermined genetic identity, subjecting him—as has been stated—to a form of biological slavery, from which it would be difficult to free himself. The fact that someone would arrogate to himself the right to determine arbitrarily the genetic characteristics of another person represents a grave offense to the dignity of that person as well as to the fundamental equality of all people . . . In the encounter with another person, we meet a human being who owes his existence and his proper characteristics to the love of God, and only the love of husband and wife constitutes a mediation of that love in conformity with the plan of the Creator and heavenly Father" (DP, no. 29).

- As for therapeutic cloning, it must be clarified that "to create embryos with the intention of destroying them, even with the intention of helping the sick, is completely incompatible with human dignity, because it makes the existence of a human being at the embryonic stage nothing more than a means to be used and destroyed. It is gravely immoral to sacrifice a human life for therapeutic ends" (DP, no. 30).

- As an alternative to therapeutic cloning, some have proposed new techniques that would be capable of producing embryonic stem cells without presupposing the destruction of true human embryos, for example through Altered Nuclear Transfer (ANT) or Oocyte Assisted Reprogramming (OAR). In this regard, however, there are still unresolved questions "regarding above all the ontological status of the 'product' obtained in this way" (DP, no. 30).

Are the following permitted?

1. The therapeutic use of stem cells

✠ "Stem cells are undifferentiated cells with two basic characteristics: a) the prolonged capability of multiplying themselves while maintaining the undifferentiated state; b) the capability of producing transitory progenitor cells from which fully differentiated cells descend, for example, nerve cells, muscle cells and blood cells.

"Once it was experimentally verified that when stem cells are transplanted into damaged tissue they tend to promote cell growth and the regeneration of the tissue, new prospects opened for regenerative medicine, which have been the subject of great interest among researchers throughout the world" (DP, no. 31).

✠ For an ethical assessment, one must consider above all the methods used for collecting stem cells.

✠ "Methods which do not cause serious harm to the subject from whom the stem cells are taken are to be considered licit. This is generally the case when tissues are taken from: a) an adult organism; b) the blood of the umbilical cord at the time of birth; c) fetuses who have died of natural causes" (DP, no. 32). "The obtaining of stem cells from a living human embryo, on the other hand, invariably causes the death of the embryo and is consequently gravely illicit. 'Research, in such cases, irrespective of efficacious therapeutic results, is not truly at the service of humanity. In fact, this research advances through the suppression of human lives that are equal in dignity to the lives of other human individuals and to the lives of the researchers themselves'" (DP, no. 32). "The use of embryonic stem cells or differentiated cells derived from them—even when these are provided by other researchers through the destruction of embryos or when such cells are commercially available—presents serious problems from the standpoint of cooperation in evil and scandal" (DP, no. 32).

✠ It should be noted, however, that numerous studies tend to produce better results with adult stem cells than with those taken from embryos.

2. Attempts at hybridization

"Recently animal oocytes have been used for reprogramming the nuclei of human somatic cells—this is generally called *hybrid cloning*—in order to extract embryonic stem cells from the resulting embryos without having to use human oocytes. From the ethical standpoint, such procedures represent an offense against the dignity of human beings on account of *the admixture of human and animal genetic elements capable of disrupting the specific identity of man*" (DP, no. 33).

For more on this topic:

> Instruction *Dignitas Personae: On Certain Bioethical Questions*, published on December 12, 2008, by the Congregation for the Doctrine of the Faith.

V
Assisted
Reproduction

What is homologous artificial insemination and fertilization?

When the spermatozoon and the ovum come from the couple itself (a man and woman united in matrimony).

And heterologous?

When the spermatozoon and/or ovum do not come from the couple united in matrimony.

What moral principles are involved in these techniques?

✠ Here are a few moral principles of a general nature that must be taken into account when expressing a moral assessment of these techniques:

- Not all that which is scientifically and technically feasible is also morally acceptable.
- It is not right to obtain something good through evil.
- The end does not justify the means. Therefore the service to life (which is done through artificial fertilization) must be realized with licit means.
- As for life (whether in birth, in life, or in death), we are neither masters nor creators, but administrators.
- The sacred context of life must be protected (above all at the time of birth and death).
- Certain fundamental rights must be respected, such as the right of the embryo to be respected and to not be an object of scientific selections or manipulations; the right of the newborn to know his or her biological parents (the right to a biological, societal, and affective identity; there are excellent reasons to defend this right of children to know their parents and to put an end to anonymous paternity); the right of women not to be considered egg-making machines or wombs for rent.
- It is necessary to enact family and health policies that represent a real and proper prevention of sterility.
- The principle must be respected that it is not in the power of human beings to establish arbitrarily that which is good or evil; and it is necessary to reject the principle of the exaltation of free will, of one's own ego, without any attention to the law of God and to the rights of the unborn child.
- The unborn child has rights that must be protected by human legislation as well, all the more so in that

the unborn belong to the category of the weak and defenseless.

■ When there is a discrepancy between divine law and human law, the Christian should follow the divine law.

✠ The techniques of artificial fertilization also involve a certain manner of understanding human nature: with these techniques, human nature is understood as a property of the subject, a mere cultural postulate, and therefore becomes subject to open negotiation, to arbitrary manipulation. According to the Christian conception, nature is normative in its essential and fundamental elements, in that it has been given by God the Creator and therefore gives a foundation to ethics and law.

For what reasons are artificial fertilization and insemination, homologous and heterologous, morally unacceptable?

Artificial fertilization and insemination are morally unacceptable in that they both

✠ Separate, in the conjugal act, the procreative meaning (openness to the transmission of life) from the unitive meaning (the mutual self-donation of the spouses). The person must not break the indissoluble connection that God has intended between the two ends of the conjugal act, unitive and procreative:

- Procreation must be the fruit of the conjugal act, through which man and woman collaborate with the power of the Creator.
- The fidelity of the spouses, in the unity of marriage, involves mutual respect for each other's right to become a father and mother only through one another.
- The child is and must be the fruit and sign of the mutual personal donation of the spouses, realized in the conjugal relationship.
- Children have the right to be conceived, carried in the womb, brought into the world and raised within the marriage. It is through sure and recognized reference to their parents that they can discover their own identity and pursue their human formation.
- Pius XII expressed all of this in 1956:

"The child is the fruit of the conjugal union, to the fullness of which contribute the organic functions and the sensible emotions connected to them. Even in the way in which a new subject is called into life, his or her dignity as a human person must be protected. A human person cannot be produced like a 'thing,' but has the right to be generated as the fruit of an act of love between two persons who have constituted a stable community. In the conjugal act, the special and complete expression of their love, the child becomes the gift that not only expresses their love, but also embodies it; all of the biological conditions of generation must be situated within the unity of this act" (Address to participants of the Second World Congress on fertility and sterility).

✠ Establish a dominion of technology over the origin and destiny of the human person. As soon as procreation is inserted into a technological-instrumental context, the result, in spite of all subjective good will, is the technological-instrumental treatment of the unborn child.

This technology of manipulation

- Distorts marriage; denigrates procreation; harms the dignity and rights of the child, who moreover is the weakest and most defenseless person; creates a baby factory; and fosters the risk of grave manipulation of life of the person
- Causes a waste of embryos (the "excess" embryos). The production of embryos is just as illicit as freezing them is. For all the more reason, so is their destruction. The embryo is a human being with all the constitutive rights of a person.
- Leads to greater guarantees for the rights of adults (who want a child at all costs) rather than those of children (who have the right to be conceived by an act of communion of conjugal love). The one most in need of guarantees on the part of society should be the child, who is the most defenseless. Minors must be protected!
- In many cases requires that the spermatozoa be obtained through masturbation, which is an immoral act
- Causes at least six practical problems:

1. The failure of this method (a success rate of only 18-20%)
2. An enormous waste of embryos (the loss of at least 80% of the embryos produced in the laboratory)
3. The high rate of abortion (the overwhelming majority of the embryos produced in the laboratory and transferred into the womb are spontaneously aborted at various stages)
4. The anthropological and affective fragmentation of the connection between sexuality and procreation (procreation: the fruit of becoming one flesh)
5. The risks of diseases and deformities (devastating damage, serious damage, substantial damage)
6. The degrading economic effects (buying and selling of ova and spermatozoa, renting of uteruses, "wild liberalism") create the risk of an economic exploitation of the unborn child

In addition to the problems already indicated for homologous fertilization, what further problems are created by heterologous fertilization?

Heterologous insemination/fertilization creates other problems that aggravate its immorality. In fact, it

- Damages the right of the child to be born from a father and mother known to him or her, bound to him or her by marriage and having the exclusive right to become parents through one another

- Does not respect the right (objective and subjective) of the unborn child to
  - Be born in a stable family
  - Know the identity of the parents and genetic makeup
  - Have an identity that is not only biological but also affective and educational, and a correspondence among these
- Renders impossible the control of the spread of genetic diseases, since the donors are anonymous
- Creates the danger of incest, on account of the fertilization of different women with semen from the same donor outside of the couple
- Fosters surrogate or substitute motherhood, which are illicit. The practice of "womb renting" overturns the natural order of procreation, which postulates the unity of the subject of the two fundamental operations that take place in human generation: conception and gestation. Unity is demanded above all by the dignity of the human being who is called to life. Surrogacy also does not permit the identifiability of the newborn. It causes the presence of third persons (this is what happens in surrogate motherhood or when a grandmother carries the child), three biological parents.
- Fosters the danger of compensation in "cold hard cash"; of yet another commercialization of the female body; and of a possible coercion and exploitation on the part of the stronger (financially and culturally

prosperous aspiring parents) against weak and isolated women

What are the possible consequences for children conceived through in vitro fertilization?

This is an important argument, because too often the child is seen as something the parents have a right to have (which has significant psychological and cultural consequences as well), while it must always be kept in mind that no person is a right for another.

There can be three levels of risk:

- The risk associated with the documented possibilities of certain health risks, which tend to be greater in children born through these techniques than in others
- The risk associated with the fact of being destined never to know the identity of one's parent, in the case of heterologous fertilization
- The risk of the possibility of being "selected to order," sometimes even choosing the birth of a child with anomalies

When is artificial insemination/fertilization morally acceptable?

✠ It is morally acceptable under three conditions:

- It must take place within a couple connected by a stable matrimonial bond.

- It must be realized through a conjugal sexual relationship, and not by collecting semen through masturbation or the avoidance of the conjugal relationship.
- It must not involve invasive or risky interventions that would harm the embryo or fetus.

✠ The common good therefore demands that the following three rights be guaranteed completely, for every single human embryo:

- The right to be treated as a subject, and not as an object
- The inviolable right to life
- The right to be born from and in a single heterosexual couple united in matrimony

Is there a right to have children?

There is no right to have children ("the child deserved, at all costs"), because they are a gift from God, the greatest gift of marriage. With the demand to have them no matter what, having prevails over being. The child is reduced to an object of scientific technology.

We are now reaching the bottom of respect for human values, when a child is "ordered and purchased," like in a doll shop, exceeding the limits that nature has imposed, arriving at an arbitrary control over the lives of others.

What can the spouses do when they do not have children?

Those who are affected by problems of infertility must be helped through ethically licit research, therapy, and medical technology.

If the gift of a child has not been granted to them, after exhausting their legitimate recourse to medicine, they can demonstrate their generosity through foster parenting or adoption, or by performing significant services on behalf of their neighbor. They thus realize a valuable spiritual fecundity, which surpasses the limits of biological infertility.

What does the Church think about the child born from artificial fertilization?

Once conceived, the child has all the rights and duties of any other person, has the same dignity, and deserves the same respect as any other human being.

For more on this topic, see the following pontifical documents:

Pope Paul VI, *Humanae Vitae*, 1968
Pope John Paul II, *Familiaris Consortio*, 1982
Catechism of the Catholic Church, nos. 2370-2379
Compendium of the CCC, nos. 498-501
Congregation for the Doctrine of the Faith, *Donum Vitae*, 1987

VI
Death Penalty

In what recent document does the Church talk about the death penalty?

It talks about it in the *Catechism of the Catholic Church* (CCC) and in the *Compendium of the CCC.*

How does it talk about the death penalty in these documents?

The following is the complete text of these sections:

✠ *Catechism of the Catholic Church* (nos. 2266-2267):

"The efforts of the state to curb the spread of behavior harmful to people's rights and to the basic rules of civil society correspond to the requirement of safeguarding the common good. Legitimate public authority has the right and duty to inflict punishment proportionate to the gravity of the offense. Punishment has the primary aim of redressing the disorder introduced by the offense. When it is willingly accepted by the guilty party, it assumes the value of expiation. Punishment then, in addition to defending public order and protecting people's safety, has a medicinal purpose: as far as possible, it must contribute to the correction of the guilty party.

"Assuming that the guilty party's identity and responsibility have been fully determined, the traditional teaching of the Church does not exclude recourse to the death penalty, if this is the only possible way of effectively defending human lives against the unjust aggressor.

"If, however, non-lethal means are sufficient to defend and protect people's safety from the aggressor, authority will limit itself to such means, as these are more in keeping with the concrete conditions of the common good and more in conformity to the dignity of the human person.

"Today, in fact, as a consequence of the possibilities which the state has for effectively preventing crime, by rendering one who has committed an offense incapable of doing harm—without definitely taking away from him the possibility of redeeming himself—the cases in which the execution of the offender is an absolute necessity 'are very rare, if not practically nonexistent.'"

✠ *Compendium of the CCC* (nos. 468-469):

"What is the purpose of punishment?

"A punishment imposed by legitimate public authority has the aim of redressing the disorder introduced by the offense, of defending public order and people's safety, and contributing to the correction of the guilty party.

"What kind of punishment may be imposed?

"The punishment imposed must be proportionate to the gravity of the offense. Given the possibilities which the State now has for effectively preventing crime by rendering one who has committed an offense incapable of doing harm, the cases in which the execution of the offender is an absolute necessity 'are very rare, if not practically non-existent' (*Evangelium Vitae*). When non-lethal means are sufficient, authority should limit itself to such means because they better correspond to the concrete conditions of the common good, are more in conformity with the dignity of the human person, and do not remove definitively from the guilty party the possibility of reforming himself."

What observations can be made about the presentation of the death penalty in these documents?

✠ In order to understand what the CCC says about the death penalty, the following fundamental elements affirmed by the CCC with regard to punishment in general must be taken into account in a unifying and complementary way.

✠ Punishment, in fact

- Must be proportionate to the seriousness of the offense
- If accepted voluntarily by the offender, takes on the value of expiation
- Has the aim of
    - Repairing the disorder introduced by the offense

- Discouraging the commission of crime
- Contributing to the correction of the offender
- Defending the public order and protecting personal safety
■ Must be inflicted by the legitimate public authority

And about the death penalty in particular?

■ The *Catechism* affirms that it is inflicted as a penalty, and therefore as a punishment, a repression of the crime, and an expiation. (In fact, it calls it *punishment*, and talks about it in the next paragraph, 2267, immediately after the one dedicated to punishment in general.)

■ At the same time, the *Catechism* expands the discussion and the context. In fact, it situates the death penalty within the wider and more positive section "Respect for Human Life" (and therefore within the Fifth Commandment: You shall not kill). And it justifies this insertion, presenting recourse to the death penalty as an application of the moral principle of *legitimate defense*, which is a grave obligation of the authority that is responsible for the lives of others.

■ Concerning the legitimate defense of persons and societies, it must be emphasized that this "is not an exception to the prohibition against the murder of the innocent that constitutes intentional killing. 'The act of self-defense can have a double effect: the preservation of one's own life; and the killing of the aggressor . . . The one is intended, the other is not.'

"Legitimate defense can be not only a right but a grave duty for one who is responsible for the lives of others. The defense of the common good requires that an unjust aggressor be rendered unable to cause harm. For this reason, those who legitimately hold authority also have the right to use arms to repel aggressors against the civil community entrusted to their responsibility" (CCC, nos. 2263, 2265).

✠ The *Catechism* also dictates the conditions for the application of the death penalty. In particular, it

- Belongs to the *traditional teaching* of the Church (see CCC, no. 2267), which has upheld the moral and legal legitimacy of the death penalty on the basis of three of its purposes: *deterrence* (intimidation or prevention), in that it discourages the commission of certain crimes; *restitution* (or retribution), in that it reestablishes a disrupted social equilibrium, restoring the balance between crime and punishment; *defense* of society from dangerous persons.
- Requires the complete ascertainment of
  - The identity
  - And the responsibility of the offender
- Must be the only practical and effective way to defend the lives of human beings from an unjust aggressor
- Must be inflicted by the legitimate public authority (excluding any form of lynching or vigilante justice)
- Must be inflicted only if the crime is proportionate to it

✠ Finally, the *Catechism* states that the necessity is very rare today, if not practically nonexistent, and gives two reasons for this:

- The greater ability the state has today to suppress crime effectively by rendering harmless the one who has committed it
- The greater quality and efficacy of nonlethal means, when these are sufficient to defend against the aggressor and protect the safety of persons. And it also presents three reasons for this: these means correspond better to the concrete conditions of the common good, they are more in keeping with the dignity of the person, and they do not definitively deprive the offender of the possibility of redemption.

✠ Thus the *Catechism*, by stating that in such a case the authority should limit itself to nonlethal means, is urging the rejection of the death penalty, which is affirmed on the level of principle but rejected at the practical level. In this sense, the *Catechism* reiterates what is affirmed in the encyclical *Evangelium Vitae* (1995), in which John Paul II writes, "In the same perspective [of hope] there is evidence of a growing public opposition to the death penalty, even when such a penalty is seen as a kind of 'legitimate defense' on the part of society. Modern society in fact has the means of effectively suppressing crime by rendering criminals harmless without definitively denying them the chance to reform" (no. 27).

✠ At the same time, the *Catechism* urges the political powers to resort to the *minimum coercion* in order to "defend and protect people's safety from the aggressor" (no. 2267). According to St. Thomas, "if a man in self-defense uses more than necessary violence, it will be unlawful" (no. 2264).

What conclusions can be drawn from this presentation of the death penalty on the part of the Church?

Since the *Catechism* has inserted the death penalty into the wider context described above, the following conclusions can be drawn:

✠ With regard to the offender:

- There must be an attempt to rehabilitate the offender even as he or she is being punished. This is better obtained by not resorting to the death penalty but offering the possibility of remaining alive in order to redeem oneself, making amends for the crime through a better conduct of life, or at least through the suffering of prison.

- It is also necessary to repair in this manner the disorder introduced by the offense. But such reparation must not be effected by shedding more blood—the death of the offender (which would imply among other things a return to the *lex talionis*: an eye for an eye, a tooth for a tooth . . .)—but by doing good (better conduct of life on the part of the offender, or at least a life of suffering in prison, in view of the hope of rehabilitation). On the other hand, isn't it possible that a long life of suffering in prison is more difficult (and therefore a more serious punishment for the offender, and also a punishment more proportionate to the seriousness of the crime) than a death that takes place in a few moments and in a state of complete or partial unconsciousness?

■ Crime must be discouraged. This is better obtained not by killing the offender, but by placing him or her in such conditions as not to cause harm again (because he or she remains in prison or has been rehabilitated).

■ It must be remembered that only God is master of life and death. Human life is sacred, because it is placed under the sovereignty of God and is therefore exempt from all human power. The life of not only the innocent person, but also the criminal, enjoys the protection of God, as God himself demonstrated when he intervened on behalf of Cain, preventing him from being killed (see Gn 4:14-15). God does not want the death of the sinner, but that such a one should convert and live.

✠ With regard to society:

■ It is indispensable to educate all to consider and evaluate the punishment inflicted on the person in the wider context of the dignity of the person (a particularly important issue today). In this sense, any punishment must be aimed at the rehabilitation of the offender. Just as any recourse to the death penalty must also be situated within the wider context of legitimate defense (which the legitimate public authority can and must use in certain cases in order to defend the lives of the persons entrusted to it) and thus, in the final analysis, of respect for the human life of others.

- There is a need to create more and more the conditions for overcoming the recourse to the death penalty, emphasizing and maximizing
  - The importance of the dignity of the human person, who can and must be better defended and prosecuted with nonlethal means
  - The greater possibilities available to the state now for deterring crime effectively by rendering harmless the one who has committed it
- It is just as necessary to make efforts to affirm the value of every human life, in all its phases, in all its moments, from conception to natural death. Unfortunately there is too often an individualism and a relativism that lead to maintaining, in a schizophrenic manner, that in some circumstances the lives of others must be maintained and protected, and in other circumstances (for example, as in the case of abortion and euthanasia), the lives of others can be legitimately destroyed, and no one must object to this.

VII
Euthanasia

What does "euthanasia" mean?

✠ It is a word with significant historical variability, with different meanings according to the use that is made of it. It can mean

- "Good death" or "without suffering," managed by the physician to reduce pain
- An action or omission that causes death with the intention of putting an end to the pain for a patient with no more hope of healing
- "Suicide by request" of the patient (assisted suicide)

✠ And yet, no matter what it is called or how it is understood, euthanasia involves bringing about the death of someone still alive, perhaps by disguising it sometimes under a veil of human kindness, a death, moreover, that is planned by the physician, who, by vocation and profession, is a minister of life.

What moral assessment must be given to euthanasia?

Various moral principles are involved in the practice of euthanasia.

✠ Euthanasia contradicts the fundamental principle of the inviolability of the right to life, a right that belongs only to God. Life is an inalienable and inviolable good in that it is a gift from God, not subject to anyone's determination or decision, including the sick person himself or herself, who retains his or her dignity fully throughout the course of life, until its natural conclusion.

✠ "Life in time can be considered a relative good only in reference to eternal life; and only in this perspective, and not with respect to other goods, can it become an instrument of a higher good, which is God himself. But it cannot be considered a relative good with respect to other human goods, because there is no human good without life. Much less can one think of creating degrees within life, by which, especially at its beginning and final moments, it could be considered in some conditions less worthy, and at most a disposable and even eliminable good" (His Excellency Giuseppe Bertori, Homily, November 20, 2008).

✠ Sharing the suicidal intention of another and helping that person through "assisted suicide" means becoming a collaborator, and sometimes a protagonist, of a culture of death, of an injustice that can never be justified, not even when it is requested.

✠ Assisted suicide, by the patient's decision and practiced by medical personnel, although permitted by the law of the state, is, to all effect

- A crime against the life of the human person
- An abdication of medical science
- A legal aberration

✠ "The request that rises from the human heart, especially when a person is tempted to cede to discouragement and has reached the point of wishing to disappear, is above all a request for company and an appeal for greater solidarity and support in trial" (Pope Benedict XVI, Address to the ambassador of Luxembourg, December 18, 2008).

✠ The effective logic of euthanasia is essentially selfish and individualistic, and as such, contradicts the logic of mutual concern and trust on which any form of coexistence is based.

✠ The individual does not have the right to determine his or her own death. There is no right to a choice between life and death.

✠ One must instead speak of a right to die well, peacefully, avoiding needless suffering. This coincides with the right to be taken care of and assisted with all ordinary means available (for example: artificial respiration, nutrition and hydration, pain treatment . . .), without resorting to treatment that is too dangerous or burdensome, and with the exclusion of any aggressive treatment. The right to die with dignity does not at all coincide with the supposed right to euthanasia, which is instead an essentially individualistic and rebellious behavior. The yes that is said to life requires the rejection of both aggressive treatment and euthanasia. And it applies to both dimensions:

- It applies to aggressive treatment, which says: "I have the power to keep death away."
- And it applies to euthanasia, which says: "I have the power to anticipate death."

Neither of these two enters into a correct logic, because both of them take the perspective: "I own life, and I am the one who decides when it must continue or when it ends."

✠ It must also be kept in mind that from a moral point of view, it is one thing to decline the start of treatment, and another to perform a positive action to interrupt it.

✠ Euthanasia originates in an ideology that claims total human power over life, and therefore over death; an ideology that absurdly entrusts to a human being the power of deciding who lives and for how long, and who does not live (eugenics).

✠ It is an extreme form of escape in the face of the anguish of death (seen as useless, meaningless). It is a shortcut that does not give any meaning to dying, nor does it confer dignity upon the dying person. It is a strategy of removal; the human person has fallen victim to fear and invokes death in spite of knowing that this is a defeat and an act of extreme weakness.

✠ It is also seen sometimes as a way to limit costs, above all with regard to the terminally ill, dementia patients, withered and unproductive elderly persons . . . dead weight for themselves, for their relatives, for the hospitals, for society . . . Euthanasia is often desired not out of the interest of the patient, but of "third parties."

✠ Those who want to die leave a stain on us, because their refusal to live is also our fault.

✠ "It is to be feared that at some point the gravely ill or elderly will be subjected to tacit or even explicit pressure to request death or to administer it to themselves" (Pope Benedict XVI, Address to the diplomatic corps of Austria, September 7, 2007).

✠ Some call for euthanasia by resorting to the principle of *quality of life*. But this principle poses various problems: by what standard of measurement and by whom is this quality *established*? Is such a criterion valid and equal for all?

✠ As for the entirely Catholic thought that even one minute more is important, one thinks of how many times the last minute has overturned the meaning of a whole existence. It happens in the lives of kings as in those of peasants. It can even happen that this is the only moment endowed with meaning. For this reason, living in a society where everyone does everything possible to help you to live is better than a society where you know that at a certain point you let yourself go, and everyone lets you go.

✠ Euthanasia also raises a series of agonizing questions that no one would be able to answer once euthanasia were legalized. Here are some of them:

- On the basis of what criterion can a subject be considered "destroyed by pain?"
- How can the state determine the intensity of suffering that is required to legitimate euthanasia?
- And who is authorized to decide yes or no: the physician, or also a friend or relative?
- What should the assessment be of the deliberate act of a physician to support a patient's will to die?
- Who guarantees that the "gentle death" has in fact been decided to put an end to a suffering seen as intolerable, and not for some other reason, perhaps out of undisclosed interests (even financial)?
- Ruling out the case of aggressive treatment, is there truly a human right to reject or suspend treatment, or not treat a sick person at all?

What is the role of the state, of the law?

✠ In euthanasia, the state, as guarantor and promoter of fundamental rights, takes on the role of "decider" of death, even if the actual execution is left to others.

✠ The state cannot limit itself to taking note of what is already present in the social mentality and practice. The modern state must confront the culture of its citizens and their needs. But it is just as true that it is not bound to accept them when they are harmful to fundamental rights.

✠ It is to be emphasized that one significant factor is the effect of approval and the ethical influence that civil legislation has on public morality. Some think: "It is the law, therefore it is permitted."

✠ If laws in favor of euthanasia are approved, these could be some of the consequences:

- A greater number of persons in our society would accept euthanasia as something normal.
- Respect for human life would continue to diminish.
- Physicians would be subjected to stronger and stronger social pressure to practice euthanasia and assisted suicide, as if it were part of their responsibility as physicians and part of their normal professional activity. Moreover, it would diminish trust in physicians.
- There would be less emotional availability to help the sick in the terminal stage to face their suffering, to alleviate and share it. It is simply absurd to eliminate the sick person because the disease cannot be eliminated!
- A climate could be created around the sick person that would make him or her feel obligated to lift from others the burden that he or she has become on account of intensive, long-term treatments.
- It would be absurd if the permission to resort to euthanasia were in time to lead to situations in which terminally ill patients, their families, and their physicians felt the need to justify their opposition to euthanasia and assisted suicide.

What must be done against the culture of death?

✠ It is necessary to

- Unite the efforts of all those who believe in the inviolability of human life, including terminal

- Resist any temptation to put an end to the life of a patient through a deliberate act of omission or an active intervention

- Reinforce hospice institutions

- Make the forms of family, civil, and religious assistance and solidarity more efficient

- Guarantee assistance that includes effective and accessible forms of treatment, pain relief, and forms of shared support. Any treatment that is ineffective or aggravates suffering is to be avoided, but also the imposition of unusual and extraordinary treatment methods.

- Offer the dying person human support. This is of fundamental importance, because the longing that arises from the human heart in the supreme confrontation with suffering and death, especially when one is tempted to fall into despair and almost to be annihilated in it, is above all a longing for companionship, for solidarity, and for support in trial.

- Destine more resources for the treatment of the incurably ill

- Promote the ethical, psychological, social, and technological formation of health care workers

- Have in particular a "good palliative assistance and a good hospitalization," which dying with human dignity requires
- Promote, in every way possible, the principle according to which death is not and cannot be at the disposal of the state or of science, or even of the individual. The attempt to eliminate illness and extreme suffering from the horizon of our lives with the shortcut of euthanasia is a risk with unforeseeable consequences.
- Pay attention to the statement of the Holy See, through the CDF, according to which "in the imminence of a death that is inevitable in spite of the means used, it is licit in conscience to make the decision to decline treatments that would produce only a precarious and distressing prolongation of life, without interrupting the normal treatment due to the sick person in such cases" (*Declaration on Euthanasia*, May 5, 1980)

✠ One must above all present the Christian conception of suffering and death.

What is the Christian conception of suffering and death?

✠ Life is a gift from God. Human beings are not the masters of their own lives, in that they are not their own creators. They receive it as a gift, just as every instant of their lives is a precious gift. Human beings administer their lives and must answer for them responsibly to the One who has given them existence.

It is therefore not the place of human beings to put an end to their own lives. Every moment of their lives, even when marked by suffering, by illness, has a meaning, a value to be appreciated and made fruitful for themselves and for others.

✠ Of course, it is right to fight against illness, because health is a gift from God. But it is also important to be able to interpret the plan of God when suffering knocks at our door. The "key" of this interpretation is constituted by the Cross of Christ. The Incarnate Word came to meet our weakness by taking it upon himself in the mystery of the Cross. Since then, all suffering has acquired a possibility of meaning that makes it uniquely precious, if it is united with the suffering of Christ.

✠ Suffering, a consequence of Original Sin, takes on, through Christ, a new meaning. It becomes a participation in the salvific work of Jesus Christ. United with that of Christ, human suffering becomes a means of salvation for oneself and for others.

Through the suffering of the Cross, Christ has prevailed over evil and also allows us to overcome it.

✠ Even the conception of death itself, from a Christian point of view, is something new and consoling.

✠ A life that is coming to an end is no less valuable than a life that is beginning. It is for this reason that the person who is dying deserves the greatest respect and the most loving care.

✠ Death, in the Christian faith, is an exodus, a passage, not the end of everything. With death, life is not taken away, but transformed. For the one who dies without mortal sin, death is entering into the communion of God's love, the fullness of life and of happiness. It is seeing his face, which is the source of light and love, precisely as a child, a newborn, sees the faces of his parents.

For this reason, the Church speaks of the death of the saint as a second birth: the definitive and eternal birth to heaven.

✠ The definitive and complete victory of Christ over evil, suffering, and death will be realized and manifested at the end of the world, when God will create new heavens and a new earth, and will be "all in all" (1 Cor 15:28).

For more on this topic, see the following pontifical documents:

> *Catechism of the Catholic Church*, nos. 2276-2279
> *Compendium of the* CCC, no. 470
> Congregation for the Doctrine of the Faith, *Declaration on Euthanasia*, 1980

VIII
Relationship of Man and Woman

What does the Church say about the relationship between man and woman?

✠ The Church, enlightened by faith in Jesus Christ, affirms

- The personal nature of the human being. Both man and woman are persons, to an equal extent.
- The equal dignity of persons, which is realized as physical, psychological, and ontological complementarity, giving rise to a harmonious relational "uni-duality." Man and woman are at the same time equal as persons and complementary as male and female. In their equality and in their difference, both have a common dignity; both are human beings to the same degree.
- The importance and the meaning of sexual difference, which is not a cultural product

- The existence of the one with and for the other (and not one against the other)
- An approach that is relational, not competitive or of rivalry
- The vocation to reciprocity, complementarity, collaboration, communion, and active cooperation between man and woman based on recognition of the intrinsic, essential, profound, and complementary difference between them
- The presence of sin, which disfigures but does not erase this positive relationship and collaboration

✠ This uni-duality of man and woman is based on the dignity of every person, created in the image and likeness of God: "Male and female he created them" (Gn 1:27). It avoids an indistinct uniformity and featureless equality as well as a gaping and conflictual difference. This dual unity, inscribed in body and soul, brings with it the relationship with the other, love for the other, interpersonal communion (see John Paul II, *Letter to Women*, no. 8).

On what does the Church base this conception?

It bases it on Sacred Scripture, which reveals the "beginning" (Mt 19:4-6)—the truth of creation and the nature of the human person—and which is also rich in human wisdom. Sacred Scripture reveals that this conception was gradually manifested through God's intervention on behalf of humanity.

How does the Old Testament present the importance of man and woman?

In various ways. For example, the Old Testament

- Presents a history of salvation that brings into play simultaneously the participation of male and female, the importance of man and woman
- Uses a nuptial vocabulary. God makes himself known as the bridegroom who loves Israel, his bride. This vocabulary touches upon the very nature of the relationship that God establishes with his people, even if this relationship is broader than what can be experienced in human marriage.
- Presents a very human love, which celebrates the beauty of the body and the happiness of mutual longing, and in which God's love for his people is also expressed (see for example Song of Songs)

And how does the New Testament present the relationship between man and woman?

The New Testament confirms and completes what is already present in the Old Testament:

- In his masculinity, Jesus Christ, the Son of God made man, assumes in his person everything that the symbolism of the Old Testament had applied to God's love for his people, described like the love of a bridegroom for his bride.

- In her femininity, the Virgin Mary, as the chosen daughter of Zion, recapitulates and transfigures the condition of Israel/Bride in anticipation of the day of its salvation.
- The beloved Spouse of Christ the Bridegroom is the Church.
- Revelation itself concludes with the words of the Bride and of the Spirit, who implore the coming of the Bridegroom: "Come, Lord Jesus" (Rev 22:20).
- The total and indissoluble love of man and woman, lived out in the power of Baptism, becomes a sacrament, a reality that manifests and communicates the love of Christ and of the Church.
- In the grace of Christ who renews their hearts, man and woman become capable of freeing themselves from sin and knowing the joy of mutual self-giving. In the power of the Resurrection of Christ, fidelity is able to overcome the weaknesses, the wounds, and the sins of the couple.
- The rivalry, enmity, and violence that disfigure the relationship of man and woman are, in Christ, able to be overcome. Their difference does not become a reason for discord to be overcome through negation or uniformity, but a possibility for cooperation that must be cultivated with mutual respect for distinction.

In the Christian understanding, what is the importance of the person's sexuality?

In the Christian understanding, sexuality is of great importance from both the basic anthropological and theological-anthropological point of view.

✠ In the light of reason (illuminated by faith), the basic anthropological dimension of sexuality

- Is the sexually distinguished humanity that is explicitly declared "image of God." Sexual identity is one's identity as a man or a woman. Sexual difference is an irreducible difference, constitutive of the human person.
- Characterizes man and woman not only on the physical level, but also on the psychological and spiritual level, leaving its imprint on everything they do
- Is a fundamental component of the personality, one of its ways of being, of manifesting itself, of communicating with others, of feeling, of expressing and experiencing human love
- Affirms the spousal nature of the body, in which the masculinity or femininity of the person is inscribed

✠ The theological-anthropological dimension of sexuality:

- The man-woman distinction is willed and created by God: "God created mankind in his image; in the image of God he created them; male and female he created them" (Gn 1:26-27).

- The relationship between man and woman is good, but it has been wounded by sin and needs to be healed: and Christ can and wants to do this.

What are the negative aspects today in the relationship between woman and man?

✠ Here are some negatives that are seen today in the relationship between man and woman:

- Subordination, which diminishes respect and cooperation
- Antagonism, rivalry
- An attitude of conflict
- Distrustful and defensive opposition
- The attempt to eliminate the differences between man and woman, starting with those of biology and sexuality, falsely considered the mere effects of historical-cultural conditioning

✠ These negative aspects must not be overgeneralized, however, and in any case can and must be overcome.

What are the consequences of obscuring this difference or duality of the sexes?

✠ It produces enormous consequences on various levels, for example:

- The bringing into question of the family, the fundamental nature of which is bi-parental, meaning made up of father and mother

- The equating of homosexuality with heterosexuality
- A new model of polymorphous sexuality
- The supposed freedom of each person to take on whatever identity he or she wishes, in both sexuality and marriage
- The insignificance of the fact that the Son of God took on human nature in its masculine form

✠ In particular, the failure to recognize the sexual difference between man and woman can even lead to a rejection of the Sacred Scriptures, which are falsely seen as transmitting a patriarchal conception of God fostered by a male chauvinist culture.

In what does the uniqueness of woman consist, according to the Christian vision?

Woman preserves the profound intuition that the best part of her life is made up of activities aimed at the awakening, the growth, the protection of the other. She points to the fundamental capacity of every human being to live for the other and because of the other. The advancement of woman in society must therefore be understood and intended as a humanization of the human person, whether man or woman, and of society itself, realized through the values rediscovered thanks to women.

How is this intuition expressed?

This intuition is connected to the physical capacity of woman to give life. Whether realized or potential, this capacity is a reality that structures the female personality at its core.

What does the biological capacity to give life make possible for woman?

✠   It allows her to reach maturity very quickly, with a sense of the gravity of life and of the responsibilities that it implies.

✠   It develops in her a respectful sense of the concrete, which is opposed to the abstractions that are often lethal to the existence of individuals and society.

✠   It is woman, finally, who even in the most desperate situations—as remote and recent history bear witness—possesses a unique capacity to withstand adversity, to make life possible even in extreme situations, to preserve a tenacious sense of the future, and to bear tribute to the value of each human life with her tears.

Should woman be considered solely under the aspect of biological procreation?

Certainly not! The very existence of the Christian vocation to virginity radically contests the presumption of confining woman to a purely biological destiny.

What is the relationship between physical motherhood and virginity?

It is a relationship of complementarity. Just as virginity receives from physical motherhood the reminder that there is no Christian vocation except in the concrete gift of oneself to the other, so likewise physical motherhood receives from virginity the reminder of its fundamentally spiritual dimension. It is not by contenting oneself with giving physical life that one truly generates the other. This means that motherhood can be fully realized even where there is no physical generation.

Pope John Paul II speaks of the genius of women. What does this uniqueness imply for the life of society?

✠ The expression "feminine genius," which John Paul II attributes to woman, indicates her capacity to "see far," "intuit," "see with the eyes of the heart."

✠ It also implies that woman is present actively and even with firmness in the family, the primordial and in a sense the sovereign society, where the person learns to be loved and to love, to be respected and to respect, to know and love God. It will be to society's credit if it makes it possible for mothers to dedicate themselves to the care and education of their children, according to their different needs according to age. And this without hampering their freedom, without psychological or practical discrimination, without penalizing them relative to their peers.

✠ It also implies that women should be present in the world of work and of social organization, and that they should have access to positions of responsibility that offer them the possibility of inspiring national policy and promoting innovative solutions to economic and social problems.

How can family and work be harmonized for women?

✠ This problem is not only legal, economic, and organizational. It is above all a problem of mentality, of culture and respect.

✠ It involves

- Labor law and organization in harmony with the demands of woman's mission within the family
- A proper appreciation of the work done by women within the family. The work of housekeeping, "starting with that of the mother, precisely because it is a service directed and devoted to the quality of life, constitutes a type of activity that is eminently personal and personalizing, and that must be socially recognized and valued, also by means of economic compensation in keeping with that of other types of work" (*Compendium of the Social Doctrine of the Church*, no. 250).
- Respect for the characteristics of women that are different from those of men
- The presence of women in the world of work and of social and political organization

What is the role of woman in the life of the Church?

✠ Women are called to be irreplaceable models and witnesses for all Christians of how the Bride (the Church) must respond with love to the love of the Bridegroom (Christ the Lord).

✠ The figure of the Virgin Mary constitutes the fundamental reference in the Church as a model of behaviors which, although typical of all the baptized, are in fact characteristic of woman, who lives them out with particular intensity and naturalness.

What are the behaviors of which Mary is the model?

✠ Mary is the model in

- Listening to and welcoming the Word of God
- Rendering praise and thanks to God for all his benefits (see Magnificat)
- Recognizing the infinite humility of God, who became man in his Son, who died on the Cross for the salvation of humanity

✠ Mary is not only the model but also the one who intercedes with God, so that every human person may resemble more and more, in holiness of life, her beloved Son Jesus.

What about men?

✠ Today there is a great need to rediscover authentic masculinity and what it means to be a man, especially to be a husband and a father. Only a man can be a husband, loving his wife as Christ loved the Church. Only a man can be a father (or spiritual father). He affirms his son and daughter in their distinct identity from their mother, and he protects them especially by loving their mother. He shows them what a real man is supposed to be and how a real man is meant to love and to serve. Holy husbands and fathers are spiritual leaders in their home, who exemplify prayerful dependence on the Lord, courage, confidence, and the fruits of the Holy Spirit. Men have much to learn from women, but women also need to learn from men. Unfortunately, men have often disappeared. Fatherlessness remains a great scourge on society.

✠ Men young and old need to set their eyes on Christ, the Son of God who became man, and specifically a man, for our sake. The witness and example of saints are also crucial, especially St. Joseph, guardian of the Holy Family and patron and protector of the Church. May more husbands and fathers look to St. Joseph! We also have more recently the courageous and holy witness of Blessed John Paul II, a great spiritual father. Blessed John Paul II's rich legacy of teaching on the human person, created male and female, remains a source that needs to be mined further to develop and encourage a greater appreciation for masculinity and Catholic manhood.

Who is greatest in the eyes of God?

The one who imitates Christ the most! And therefore the one who is holiest is also the greatest on earth and in heaven!

And this is the best goal for both woman and man, without distinction.

For more on this topic:

> Congregation for the Doctrine of the Faith, *Letter to the Bishops of the Catholic Church on the Collaboration of Men and Women in the Church and in the World*, 2004

IX
What Is Love?

Some of the main points of the encyclical *Deus Caritas Est* by Pope Benedict XVI are presented here.

What do people think about love?

✠ Virgil rightly states in the *Eclogues*: "Love conquers all" (*omnia vincit amor*), and adds: "*Et nos cedamus amori*" (and we give in to love).

✠ Dante, in his *Divine Comedy*, affirms that it is "love that moves the sun and the other stars" (*Paradiso*, XXXIII, v. 145). In Dante, light and love are one and the same: they are the primordial creative power that moves the universe.

✠ Today the term "love" has become one of the most used and also abused words, to which we attach completely different meanings. One speaks of love of country, of one's profession, of love among friends, between parents and children, among brothers and relatives, of love for one's neighbor, and love for God.

✠ Although it has multiple and diverse meanings and interpretations

- The word "love" is "a fundamental word, an expression of the primordial reality. We cannot simply abandon it, but we must take it up again, purify it and bring it to its original splendor so that it can illumine our life and guide it on the right path" (Pope Benedict XVI, Address, January 23, 2006).
- The love between man and woman emerges as the archetype of love par excellence, next to which all other kinds of love appear to pale in comparison. Body and soul contribute seamlessly to the realization of this love, and the human being is presented with a promise of happiness that seems irresistible.

What objections about love are posed to the Church?

✠ Some object: Doesn't the Church perhaps

- With its commandments and prohibitions embitter the most beautiful thing in life, which is love?
- Condemn *eros* (the love of attraction) to accept only *agape* (the love of disinterested dedication)?
- Take an adversarial approach to the body, to human sexuality?
- Present a message, that of love, which today is outdated and ineffective?

In fact, we live today in an age in which

- Hostility and greed seem to have become all-powerful
- We are witnessing the apotheosis of hatred and revenge, which are sometimes associated with the name of God himself

✠ To these objections, the pope responds in the various pages of the encyclical, developing the theme of love.

What is the origin of love?

In the Christian conception, love comes from God, or rather God himself is love. Love is his *modus existendi*. "God is love, and whoever remains in love remains in God and God in him" (1 Jn 4:16). Saying that "God is love" is the same thing as saying that God loves.

What are the dimensions of love?

"Love" has three dimensions or manifestations: *eros*, *philia*, and *agape* (*caritas*).

What are the characteristics of *eros*?

✠ *Eros* has these main characteristics:

- It signifies "worldly" love.
- It is rooted in human nature itself.
- In the Bible, it has its origin in the goodness of the Creator.

- It has the aim of lifting us up "in ecstasy" toward the divine, of carrying us beyond ourselves.
- It can be degraded to pure "sex," a commodity, a mere "thing" that can be bought and sold. In that case
  - There is a degradation of the human body, which is no longer integrated into the comprehensive freedom of our existence. It is no longer a living expression of the totality of our being but is rejected in the purely biological field.
  - The human being becomes a commodity, is deprived of dignity and dehumanized.

✠ *Eros* requires a journey of ascesis, of renunciation, of purification and healing. It requires discipline and purification in order to give the person, not the pleasure of the moment, but a certain foretaste of the summit of existence, of that beatitude toward which our whole being tends.

✠ It is only in this way that *eros* can become *agape*: in this way, love for the other no longer seeks itself, but becomes concern for the other, a willingness to sacrifice for the other, and also an openness to the gift of a new human life.

What is meant by *philia*?

Philia signifies the love of friendship. It is used in the Gospel of John to express the relationship between Jesus and his disciples.

What are the characteristics of love understood as *agape* (*caritas*)?

Love understood as *agape*

- Is an ablative love: love becomes care of the other and for the other. It no longer seeks itself or the intoxication of happiness; it seeks instead the good of the beloved. It becomes renunciation, it is ready for sacrifice, even seeking it out. The happiness of the other becomes more important than my own. Then there is no longer the desire only to take, but to give, and precisely in this liberation from the ego human beings discover themselves and become full of joy.

- Is "ecstasy," not in the sense of a moment of intoxication, but ecstasy as a journey, as the permanent exodus from the ego closed in on itself to its liberation in the gift of self, and precisely in this way to the rediscovery of self, or rather to the discovery of God: "Whoever seeks to preserve his life will lose it, but whoever loses it will save it" (Lk 17:33), Jesus says.

- Is not only a feeling. Feelings come and go. It is also a feeling, but not only that. It involves all the dimensions and manifestations of the person. Love also involves the will and the intelligence. With his word, God addresses himself to our intelligence, to our will, and to our emotions in order that we may learn to love him "with all our heart and all our soul."

- Seeks definitiveness, in a twofold sense: in the sense of exclusivity ("only this one person") and in the sense of "forever." Love includes the totality of existence in every one of its dimensions, including that of time. It could not be otherwise, because his promise aims at the definitive: love aims at eternity.

■ Is not something extraneous, placed beside or even against *eros*, but *eros* and *agape* are united

How are *eros* and *agape* united?

✠ "Love" is a single reality, although it has different dimensions; from time to time, one or another dimension can emerge more prominently. In reality, *eros* and *agape* never allow themselves to be completely separated from the other. *Eros* and *agape* are not in opposition but harmonize with each other. They demand never to be completely separated from each other, but rather both, although in different dimensions, find their proper equilibrium the more the true nature of love is realized.

✠ Even if *eros* is at first desirous and yearning—a fascination with the great promise of happiness—in drawing closer to the other, it then makes fewer and fewer demands for itself, always seeking the happiness of the other first, becoming ever more concerned about the other, giving itself and desiring "to be for" the other. Thus the moment of *agape* takes root in it; otherwise *eros* decays and even loses its own nature. On the other hand, human beings cannot live exclusively in self-giving, descending love. They cannot only and always give, they must also receive. Those who want to give love must also receive it as a gift.

✠ The Fathers of the Church saw the story of Jacob's ladder as symbolic of this unbreakable bond between ascent and descent, between the *eros* that seeks God and the *agape* that transmits the gift received (see Gn 28:12; Jn 1:51).

✠ Therefore the love between man and woman that initially appears as *eros* above all must be transformed within them into *agape*, into the gift of self for the other, and this precisely in order to respond to the true nature of *eros*.

✠ In monogamous marriage, which corresponds to the image of the monotheistic God, there shines the encounter of *eros* with *agape*. Marriage based on an exclusive and definitive love becomes the icon of God's relationship with his people, and vice versa: God's way of loving becomes the measure of human love. This close connection in the Bible among *eros*, *agape*, and marriage has almost no parallel in the literature outside of it.

What places does *agape* occupy in Christianity?

It is the foundation and the center of the Christian faith. In fact:

✠ God creates everything out of love.

✠ The human being above all is created by God-Love, is created to be loved, and is created with the capacity to love. To say that we are created in the image of God means that we resemble God in love.

✠ God loves human beings gratuitously and loves them in infinite ways. In fact, God

- Is more intimate to me than I am to myself, knows me better than I know myself
- Forgives the sins of human beings
- Gives them the Holy Spirit, who is Love
- Becomes man himself in Jesus Christ, so that human beings may become children of God

✠ Jesus Christ

- Is the One in whom God has taken on a human face and a human heart
- Is the Love that gives itself even unto death. He dies and rises from the dead in order to save humanity.
- Even becomes our food in the Eucharist. What had once been standing in the presence of God now becomes, through participation in the self-donation of Jesus, the participation in his Body and Blood, an intimate and profound union with him.
- While binding us to him, also unites us among ourselves, making us into one big family: the Church. "Because the loaf of bread is one, we, though many, are one body, for we all partake of the one loaf," St. Paul says (1 Cor 10:17).

✠ In Christianity, *agape*

- Is the greatest reality. "The greatest of these is love" (1 Cor 13:13). The Law of Moses contains 613 precepts and prohibitions. How is one to discern which is the greatest of all of these? Jesus responds readily: "You shall love the Lord, your God, with all your heart, with all your soul, and with all your mind. This is the greatest and the first commandment . . . The whole law and the prophets depend on these two commandments" (Mt 22:37-38, 40).

- Is at the origin of the human identity. "Being Christian is not the result of an ethical choice or a lofty idea, but the encounter with an event, a person, which gives life a new horizon and a decisive direction" (*Deus Caritas Est*, no. 1).

- Impacts the personal, social, and cultural levels, proposing a style of life that breaks the circle of superficiality and egotism in which we are confined

- Leads us to consider the human person "a unity in duality, a reality in which spirit and matter compenetrate, and in which each is brought to a new nobility" (*Deus Caritas Est*, no. 5)

- "Does not eliminate legitimate differences, but harmonizes them in a superior unity that is not ordered from the *outside* but gives form from *within*, so to speak, to the whole" (Benedict XVI, Homily, January 25, 2006)

- Fuses together the love of God and love of neighbor. In the least we encounter Jesus himself, and in Jesus we encounter God. I also love, in God and with God, the person I do not like or even know. He wants us to become friends of his friends. "'Worship' itself,

Eucharistic communion, includes the reality both of being loved and of loving others in turn. A Eucharist which does not pass over into the concrete practice of love is intrinsically fragmented" (*Deus Caritas Est*, no. 14).

✠ Human beings can realize *agape* in that they

- Are created in the image of God-Love and are loved by God, and therefore love in the completeness of their potentialities
- Receive the gift of the Holy Spirit with Baptism and Confirmation

✠ *Agape* involves a journey of growth that "is never 'finished' and complete; throughout life, it changes and matures, and thus remains faithful to itself" (*Deus Caritas Est*, no. 17). Love, in fact, is not found already fully formed, but grows; in a manner of speaking we can learn it slowly in such a manner that it may always embrace all our powers and open for us the way to an upright life.

✠ To Dostoyevsky's question, "What is the beauty that will save the world?", the answer is: the overwhelming beauty of the Love of God.

✠ Here is a summary of some of the characteristics of Christian *agape*:

- For Christians the source and example of love of God and neighbor is the love of Christ for his Father, for humanity and for each person.

- "God is love" (1 Jn 4:16) and "God so loved the world that he gave his only Son, so that everyone who believes in him might not perish but might have eternal life" (Jn 3:16).

- God's love is placed in the human heart through the Holy Spirit.

- It is God who first loves us, thereby enabling us to love him in return.

- Love does not harm one's neighbor but rather seeks to do to the other what one would want done to oneself (see 1 Cor 13:4-7).

- Love is the foundation and sum of all the commandments (see Gal 5:14).

- Love of neighbor cannot be separated from love of God, because it is an expression of our love for God. This is the new commandment, "love one another as I love you" (Jn 15:12).

- Grounded in Christ's sacrificial love, Christian love is forgiving and excludes no one; it therefore also includes one's enemies. It should be not just words but deeds (see 1 Jn 4:18). This is the sign of its genuineness. (Final declaration of the first seminar of the Catholic-Muslim Forum, November 6, 2008)

Can love be commanded?

"Since God has first loved us (cf. 1 Jn 4:10), love is now no longer a mere 'command'; it is the response to the gift of love with which God draws near to us. . . . The 'commandment' of love is only possible because it is more than a requirement. Love can be 'commanded' because it has first been given" (*Deus Caritas Est*, nos. 1, 14).

"Love cannot be commanded. . . . God does not demand of us a feeling which we are incapable of producing. He loves us, he makes us see and experience his love, and since he has 'loved us first,' love can also blossom as a response within us" (*Deus Caritas Est*, nos. 16, 17). In Christianity, love is not an imposition, but a proposition, an example. A gift can be accepted or rejected. But the greatness of Christ is: I am here for those who want me.

Giving therefore presupposes receiving: what allows us to love is the fact that we have been loved. Our loving is the response to the gift of love with which God comes to meet us. Just as children are able to love as adults if they have been loved by their mothers and fathers, so also human beings are able to love because they have first experienced the love of God.

Is it truly possible to love God without seeing him?

✠ "True, no one has ever seen God as he is. And yet God is not totally invisible to us; he does not remain completely inaccessible. God loved us first, says the Letter of John quoted above (cf. 4:10), and this love of God has appeared in our midst. He has become visible in as much as he 'has sent his only Son into the world, so that we might live through him'

(1 Jn 4:9). God has made himself visible: in Jesus we are able to see the Father (cf. Jn 14:9)" (*Deus Caritas Est*, no. 17).

✠ We are able to love God because he did not remain at an unreachable distance but has entered and enters into our lives. He comes to us, to each one of us

- With his Word, contained in Sacred Scripture
- In the sacraments, through which he acts in our lives, especially in the Eucharist
- In the liturgy of the Church, in its prayer
- In the living community of believers: in it, we experience the love of God, we perceive his presence, and we also learn in this way to recognize it in our daily lives
- In the encounter with our neighbor, in particular with persons who have been touched by him and transmit his light
- In the events through which he intervenes in our lives
- In the signs of creation, which he has given us

✠ God has not only offered us love but has lived it out first and fully, and knocks at our hearts in so many ways to solicit our love in response.

Does faith diminish the human capacity for love?

Not at all. On the contrary, it increases it. Faith teaches us to love beyond the limits that history, culture, politics, and character impose on our relationships with others. Through the faith, we learn to look at the other person not only with our own eyes and our own feelings but according to the perspective of Jesus Christ. Every believer in Christ can love better, and more.

Those who grow closer to God do not withdraw from human beings, but instead make themselves truly close to them.

What is our model of *agape*?

✠ Jesus Christ is our model par excellence.

He is, in fact, the incarnate love of God. In him, *eros-agape* reaches its most radical form. In his Death on the Cross, Jesus, giving himself in order to lift up and save humanity, expresses love in its most sublime form, in that it accomplishes that turning to God and away from self in which he gives himself in order to lift up and save humanity.

✠ Jesus has guaranteed this act of offering a lasting presence through the institution of the Eucharist, in which, under the species of bread and wine, he gives himself as the new manna that unites us to him. By participating in the Eucharist, we too are caught up in the dynamic of his self-donation. We unite ourselves with him, and at the same time we unite ourselves with all others to whom he gives himself; all of us thus become "one body." In this way, love of God and love of neighbor are truly fused together.

Why does the Church perform the service of charity?

✠ The service of charity belongs to the essence of the Church, like the service of the sacraments and the service of the proclamation of the Gospel. These three forms of service presuppose each other and cannot be separated from one another.

✠ The Church can never be exempted from the exercise of charity as an activity organized by believers, and, on the other hand, there will never be a situation in which the charity of each individual Christian is not required, because human beings, in addition to justice, will always need love.

✠ The ecclesial organization of charity is not a form of social assistance that is casually added to the reality of the Church, an initiative that could be left to others as well. It is instead part of the nature of the Church. Just as human proclamation, the word of faith, corresponds to the divine Logos, so also the *agape* of the Church, its charitable activity, corresponds to the *Agape* that is God.

✠ Love of neighbor is a duty of every believer, as also of the entire Church community on all levels: local community (parish), particular Church (diocese), universal Church. The totally personal act of *agape* can never remain a purely individual matter but must also become an essential act of the Church as community: that is, it also needs the institutional form that is expressed in the community action of the Church.

✠ The awareness of this charitable duty has been of essential relevance in the Church from the beginning (see Acts 2:44-45), and very soon the need was shown for a certain organization as a condition for its more effective fulfillment. And so in the fundamental structure of the Church there emerged the "diaconate" as a service of love of neighbor, exercised as a community and in orderly fashion, a concrete service but at the same time spiritual (see Acts 6:1-6). With the progressive spread of the Church, this exercise of charity was confirmed as one of its essential domains (see Synthesis of the encyclical letter *Deus Caritas Est*, January 25, 2006).

Is the charitable activity of the Church contrary to justice?

✠ "Since the nineteenth century, a fundamental objection has been raised against the charitable activity of the Church; this is in opposition—it is said—to justice and would end up working as a system to preserve the status quo. With the performance of individual works of charity, the Church is seen as fostering the continuation of the current unjust system, making it bearable to some extent and thus stopping rebellion and upheaval for the sake of a better world."

✠ In response to these objections, it must be said that

- We must work constantly so that everyone has what is necessary and no one suffers from misery
- The egotism of individual persons, of groups, of nations is always lying in wait, and therefore we must constantly fight against it
- In addition to justice, human beings will always need love, which is the only thing that gives justice a soul

Can't the Church leave this service to other philanthropic organizations?

The answer is: no, the Church cannot do this. It must practice love of neighbor as a community as well, otherwise it proclaims the God of love in an incomplete and insufficient way. "Charitable commitment has a meaning that goes well beyond simple philanthropy. It is God himself who moves us interiorly to relieve misery. And so, after all, it is he himself whom we bring to the suffering world. The more consciously and clearly we bring him as a gift, the more effectively will our love change the world and reawaken hope: a hope that goes beyond death" (Pope Benedict XVI, Address, January 23, 2006).

What are the characteristics of the charitable activity of the Church?

The charitable activity of the Church, to be authentic and effective

✠ Protects its identity. It, in fact, "beyond the first very concrete meaning of helping one's neighbor, also essentially means that of communicating to others God's love, which we ourselves have received. It must make the living God in some way visible. In charitable organization, God and Christ must not be foreign words; in reality, they indicate the original source of ecclesial charity. The strength of *Caritas* depends on the strength of the faith of all the members and collaborators" (Pope Benedict XVI, Address, January 23, 2006).

The charitable activity of the Church must therefore not be diluted into a generic organization assistance.

✠ Is based on, in addition to professional competency, the experience of a personal encounter with Christ, whose love has touched the heart of the believer, eliciting love of neighbor. The program of the Christian is the program of Jesus: a heart that sees. This heart sees where there is a need for love and acts accordingly.

✠ Takes as its Magna Carta the hymn to charity of St. Paul (see 1 Cor 13f.), which prevents the risk of degrading into pure activism

✠ Is necessarily accompanied by prayer. "When we consider the immensity of others' needs, we can, on the one hand, be driven towards an ideology that would aim at doing what God's governance of the world apparently cannot: fully resolving every problem. Or we can be tempted to give in to inertia, since it would seem that in any event nothing can be accomplished. At such times, a living relationship with Christ is decisive if we are to keep on the right path, without falling into an arrogant contempt for man, something not only unconstructive but actually destructive, or surrendering to a resignation which would prevent us from being guided by love in the service of others. Prayer, as a means of drawing ever new strength from Christ, is concretely and urgently needed. People who pray are not wasting their time, even though the situation appears desperate and seems to call for action alone" (*Deus Caritas Est*, no. 36).

✠ Is realized in communion with the bishops. Without this connection, the major charitable agencies of the Church could be in danger, in practice, of dissociating themselves from the Church and identifying themselves as non-governmental bodies, like any common organization of assistance. In such a case, their philosophy could not be distinguished from the Red Cross or a UN agency.

✠ Is independent of parties and ideologies. The charitable activity of the Church "is not a means of changing the world ideologically, and it is not at the service of worldly stratagems, but it is a way of making present here and now the love which man always needs" (*Deus Caritas Est*, no. 31).

✠ Cultivates a fruitful relationship with the various charitable and philanthropic organizations, with national structures, and with the humanitarian associations that support in various ways the solidarity expressed by civil society. "The Church, through her many institutions and works, together with many other associations in your country, often attempts to deal with immediate needs, but it is the State as such which must enact laws in order to eradicate unjust structures" (Pope Benedict XVI, Address, September 12, 2008).

✠ Avoids proselytism. "Love is free; it is not practiced as a way of achieving other ends. But this does not mean that charitable activity must somehow leave God and Christ aside. For it is always concerned with the whole man. Often the deepest cause of suffering is the very absence of God. Those who practice charity in the Church's name will never seek to impose the Church's faith upon others. They realize that a pure and generous love is the best witness to the God in whom we believe and by whom we are driven to love. A Christian knows when it is time to speak of God and when it is better to say nothing and to let love alone speak. He knows that God is love (cf. 1 Jn 4:8) and that God's presence is felt at the very time when the only thing we do is to love" (*Deus Caritas Est*, no. 31).

For more on this topic:

Pope Benedict XVI *Deus Caritas Est*, 2006

X
Human Sexuality

What is the human importance of sexuality?

✠   Already on the human level, sexuality is very important in the person. In fact:

- Sexuality is an element of personal *being*. It is a structural feature. It characterizes the being of the person and actualizes it in the relational dimension for the other: to be *with and for* the other.
- Sex constitutes a natural and biological characteristic; it is not a cultural option, not a "free" choice of each person. The predominantly biological anchoring of sexual differentiation is essential, not a limitation, but rather a source of significance. If sexual identity were defined solely by culture, it would be susceptible to being transformed at will, according to individual desire or historical and social influences.
- Man and woman are by nature oriented to one another. Their otherness and originality allow reciprocity and integration.

- The sexual nature of the human being and the human faculty of procreation "wonderfully exceed the dispositions of lower forms of life" (*Gaudium et Spes*, no. 51).

- "Sexuality affects all aspects of the human person in the unity of his body and soul. It especially concerns affectivity, the capacity to love and to procreate, and in a more general way the aptitude for forming bonds of communion with others" (CCC, no. 2332).

- The human person, in the judgment of the scientists of our time, is so profoundly influenced, in every one of its expressions, by sexuality, that this must be considered as one of the factors that give rise to each of the main traits that distinguish it. From sex, in fact, the human person derives the characteristics that on the biological, psychological, and spiritual level so powerfully shape the course of its development to maturity and its insertion into society.

- Sexuality, with its manifestations, is situated at the intersection between the biological and psychological, between nature and culture, between personal identity—the anthropological significance of which is enormous—and its natural and cultural conditions.

- At the same time, the human person cannot be reduced to his or her own sexuality (sexual identity) as male or female, as if one's sexual identity exhausts the unique mystery of the person. Sexual identity is constitutive, though not exhaustive, of the person.

✠ So sexuality is not

- An accidental or secondary aspect of the personality
- A cultural or social construct
- A fleeting, transitory element

✠ Sexuality is differentiated in man (masculinity) and woman (femininity):

- The difference between man and woman is an essential element of the person, a constituent element of personal identity. The male or female sexual identity, as the ontological specificity of the individual, belongs to the unique and unrepeatable character of the human person and characterizes it in its various dimensions.
- The sexual differences between man and woman, although they certainly manifest themselves in physical attributes, in fact transcend the purely physical and touch upon the very mystery of the person, body and soul. Every person is defined (consitutively, not exhaustively) by his or her sexual identity. The person is male or female from conception, and is so in an irreversible manner, in that his or her genotype, meaning the complex of genetic characteristics of an individual, is found in all of the cells of his or her body.

How does the Christian faith view sexuality?

✠ The Christian faith welcomes and completes all of the positive aspects that already characterize the person sexually on the human level. In particular, the Christian faith makes a close association between sexuality and a certain conception and realization of love: "The person is thus capable of a higher kind of love than concupiscence, which only sees objects as a means to satisfy one's appetites; the person is capable rather of friendship and self-giving, with the capacity to recognize and love persons for themselves. Like the love of God, this is a love capable of generosity. One desires the good of the other because he or she is recognized as worthy of being loved. This is a love which generates communion between persons, because each considers the good of the other as his or her own good. This is a self-giving made to one who loves us, a self-giving whose inherent goodness is discovered and activated in the communion of persons and where one learns the value of loving and of being loved" (Pontifical Council for the Family, *The Truth and Meaning of Human Sexuality*, no. 9).

✠ Moreover, the importance of sexuality has an even more solid foundation in the Christian vision. In fact:

- The difference between the sexes belongs to the specific way in which the *Imago Dei* exists. Being in the image of God is manifested, from the beginning of human history, in sexual difference. "God created mankind in his image; in the image of God he created them; male and female he created them" (Gn 1:27).
- When a man and a woman in marriage unite their bodies and spirits in an attitude of total openness and self-donation, they reflect in some way the image of God as a communion of persons. Their union in one

flesh does not simply correspond to a biological need but to the intention of the Creator that leads them to share the happiness of being made in his image.

- Sexual specificity, in the human person, is reinforced by the Incarnation of the Word. He has assumed the human condition in its totality, taking on a sex, but becoming man in both senses of the term: as a member of the human community and as a being of the male sex.

- Christianity appreciates the corporeal human dimension in that it expresses, through corporeality, its mysteries, like those of the Incarnation and Resurrection of Christ.

- The faithful are aware of belonging to the mystical Body of Christ through their own person.

- The Incarnation and Resurrection of Christ even extend to eternity the original sexual identity of the *Imago Dei*. The Risen Lord remains a man; the sanctified and glorified person of the Mother of God, now assumed bodily into heaven, continues to be a woman.

✠ This human-Christian conception of sexuality prevents

- Persons from being *used* as things. The objectification and sexualization of the image of the human body encourages persons to treat others as something to be consumed for their sexual pleasure.

- The separation of procreation and sex, rejecting contraception on the one hand, because it separates sex from procreation, and artificial insemination on the other, because it separates procreation from sex

- Sexuality from being considered a dimension completely outside of the moral norms, where there are no values at stake but only personal tastes about which no one is permitted to express moral judgments. The claim of placing sexuality outside of and above any moral order, in a sphere of intangible rights, is the result of a radical culture, of an extreme individualism in which values become the exclusive product of an erroneous conception of individual freedom.

Is one of the sexes superior to the other?

✠ The Bible does not provide any support for the concept of a natural superiority of one sex with respect to the other. In spite of their differences, the two sexes enjoy equal dignity.

- "In creating the human race 'male and female' (Gn 1:27), God gives man and woman an equal personal dignity, endowing them with the inalienable rights and responsibilities proper to the human person" (Pope John Paul II, *Familiaris Consortio*, no. 22). Man and woman are equally created in the image of God.
- Both are persons, endowed with intelligence and will, capable of freely directing their own lives.

✠ There is an equality of the sexes in distinction, reciprocity, and complementarity:

- Each one realizes his or her sexual identity in a unique manner.
- Man and woman need each other in order to attain a fullness of life.

✠ We must appreciate the originality and specificity of man and woman in the family, in society, in the Church.

✠ The original friendship and harmony between man and woman has been seriously compromised by sin, as has the realization of the positive aspects of the human body.

What are the positive aspects of the human body?

✠ The Christian faith has a positive conception of the body, due to the fact that the body

- Is a gift of God the Creator
- Has been taken on by Christ in the Incarnation
- Is the means of redemption (the immolated and Risen Body of Christ)
- Is the temple of the Holy Spirit
- Is called to rise at the end of this world

✠ The Christian faith affirms that the human being

- Does not have physicality as an addition to human nature but as an essential part of it
- Is a unity of soul and body, as an incarnate spirit
- Is called to love as an incarnate spirit, meaning soul and body in the unity of person. Human love embraces

the body as well, and the body also expresses spiritual love. Sexuality is therefore not purely biological but concerns the profound essence of the person. The use of sexuality as physical donation has its truth and attains its full meaning when it is an expression of the personal donation of man and woman until death.

✠ At the same time, the Christian is aware that at the origin of the world is *Original Sin*, which wounded the positive aspects of the body. And therefore since that time, these positive aspects are for the person a project to be realized, including with effort and renunciation. And nonetheless it is not an impossible project, in that Christ has come to make the realization of this project possible.

What is the project of the body that is to be realized?

The awareness of having been created by God in his image and likeness leads the person to the awareness of being a *gift* received from an Other. From this *being-gift* stems the commitment, the project of *must-be-gift* with and for the other, through self-mastery and self-donation. In this way the spousal nature of the body is realized, meaning the capacity to express love: precisely that love in which the human person becomes gift and—through this gift—realizes the very meaning of being and existence.

What is the Church's view on masturbation?

✠ The Catholic Church affirms that "masturbation is an intrinsically and seriously disordered act. The main reason is that, whatever the motive for acting this way, the deliberate use of the sexual faculty outside normal conjugal relations essentially contradicts the finality of the faculty" (CDF, *Persona Humana*, no. 9).

✠ In masturbation, "sexual pleasure is sought outside of 'the sexual relationship which is demanded by the moral order and in which the total meaning of mutual self-giving and human procreation in the context of true love is achieved'" (*Persona Humana*, no. 9).

"To form an equitable judgment about the subjects' moral responsibility and to guide pastoral action, one must take into account the affective immaturity, force of acquired habit, conditions of anxiety or other psychological or social factors that lessen, if not even reduce to a minimum, moral culpability" (CCC, no. 2352).

What is the main criterion of the morality of the sexual act?

It is respect for the finality (purpose or end) of this act, within the context of conjugal love, that guarantees its moral integrity.

What is the purpose or end of the sexual act?

✠ The sexual act has two meanings to be realized: unitive and procreative. These meanings, as explained below, can only be realized in marriage.

- The unitive meaning emphasizes that the sexual act inseparably involves both personal dimensions: the physical and the spiritual. In the gift of the body, man and woman, as husband and wife, recognize and accept one another as donation and welcome, as integral and definitive communion.

  Man and woman express, in an exclusive way, the reciprocal and disinterested gift of a certain kind of love: the total, faithful, and indissoluble love for one another. Since the sexual relationship involves all dimensions of the person (physical, emotional, spiritual . . .), it also involves all of these characteristics of love.

- At the same time, the procreative meaning expresses openness to the gift of life: the child, welcomed as person, gift, promise, responsibility.

  Conjugal love, of its very nature, is fruitful. Even when a husband and a wife are not able to conceive, their love is called to be fruitful, and their acts of love in the marital embrace remain procreative-in-kind, that is, the kind of acts apt for procreation, open to the gift of life.

✠ There is an indissoluble bond between the two meanings of the sexual act, which God has willed and which no human being may presume to break. In fact, because of its profound nature, the sexual (or more properly, conjugal) act, while it unites the spouses with the deepest of bonds, makes them capable of generating new life, according to laws written in the very nature of man and woman.

✠ "If each of these essential qualities, the unitive and the procreative, is preserved, the use of marriage fully retains its sense of true mutual love and its ordination to the supreme responsibility of parenthood to which man is called" (Pope Paul VI, *Humanae Vitae*, no. 12).

The attempt to separate the exercise of sexuality from its responsible openness to life, like the symmetrically antithetical attempt to uproot human procreation from the spousal context between man and woman, constitutes a grave injury to the truth of love and to the dignity of the person.

Why does the Christian faith allow the sexual act only within the context (or covenant) of marriage?

✠ The Christian faith allows the sexual act only within the covenant of marriage because it is only in marriage that the two meanings of the sexual act, understood properly as the conjugal act, can be realized fully and inseparably. Outside of marriage, the sexual act does not realize, or realizes only partially, the richness and beauty of these meanings, and it cannot speak the language of complete self-gift, becoming, as it were, a lie to one another.

✠ The splendor and exclusivity of conjugal love stem from its fundamental qualities: humanity (sensible and spiritual), freedom, sacrifice, totality, unity, social and ecclesial status, fidelity, indissolubility, fecundity, sacramentality.

✠ It is to this conjugal love, and only to this, that sexual self-donation belongs, which is realized in a truly human way only if it is an integral part of the love with which man and woman commit themselves to each other until death.

✠ In order to realize this objective, Christian spouses can count on the divine grace that is proper and specific to the Sacrament of Matrimony. But the personal commitment of the spouses is also necessary. This is why this objective is not always realized.

✠ But when the two spouses respect and pursue the two meanings of their conjugal relationship, they

- Praise and thank God
- Bless him
- Manifest and incarnate the disinterested, faithful, and indissoluble love of God
- Sanctify one another
- Make their family, the Church, and humanity grow in holiness

✠ Sexual acts, when they are performed as conjugal acts within the Sacrament of Matrimony with respect for the unitive and procreative meanings, are a reflection of the love of the Trinity: "God, who is love and life, has inscribed in man and woman the vocation to share in a special way in his mystery of personal communion and in his work as Creator and Father" (CDF, *Donum Vitae*, Introduction, no. 3).

What is the importance of abstaining from the sexual act outside of marriage, and sometimes even within marriage?

✠ It is important not so much in its aspect of renunciation, of sacrifice, as of respect for one's own sexuality, considered and lived out in the human-Christian dimensions and values described above. Sex only makes sense within marriage, wherein the complete gift of self is possible. Sex outside of marriage is a falsification of the language of the body, which is meant to speak the full gift of self. Outside of marriage, there is no full commmitment or complete gift of self. In this way, sex becomes, as it were, a lie to oneself and to the other.

✠ Within marriage, abstaining from sexual relations (continence), in addition to reasons associated with responsible parenthood and the just use of natural methods of family planning (ferility awareness), can also

- Be an authentic sign of attention, respect, authentic and full love of the other
- Offer a therapeutic service, which means that it can offer valid assistance to live out the sexual act within marriage with greater dedication and intensity of love. The wait can increase, purify, and perfect the desire for mutual self-donation, and develop honest and chaste marital expressions of affection.

- Carry out an educational function. It can be good training for respecting conjugal fidelity within marriage, above all during the periods of the temporary and/or prolonged absence of one's spouse, or during times of unreadiness or illness on the part of one or the other.

- Foster knowledge and mastery of self, which confers a higher human value on the person. This indeed demands constant effort, but thanks to its beneficial influence, the person can develop his or her overall personality, enriching it with spiritual values. This brings fruits of serenity and peace, makes the solution of other problems easier, fosters attentiveness to the other, helps to banish egoism, the enemy of true love, and deepens the sense of responsibility.

"Indeed it is through chastity that we are gathered together and led back to the unity from which we were fragmented into multiplicity" (St. Augustine, *Confessions*, 10, 29, 40).

✠ But if it is important to abstain from the sexual act for the aforementioned reasons, it is also important to live sexuality in chastity. In fact, abstinence and self-control make up only a part of the virtue of chastity.

What is chastity?

✠ Chastity is the glorious affirmation of those who are able to live the gift of self, free from any slavery to the ego. It makes the personality harmonious, mature, full of inner peace. It makes us capable of respecting others, because it reveals them to us as persons to be venerated in that they are created in the image of God and are by grace children of God, recreated by Christ, "who called you out of darkness into his wonderful light" (1 Pt 2:9).

✠ Chastity is like transparency, and at the same time, the protection of a precious gift received—that of love, in view of the gift of self that is realized in the specific vocation of each one. Chastity is therefore that spiritual energy that is able to defend love from the dangers of egoism and aggressiveness, and to advance it toward its full realization.

✠ Chastity is not only a moral virtue (formed by love) but is equally a virtue connected with the gifts of the Holy Spirit, above all with the gift of respect for that which comes from God (*donum pietatis*).

Why is chastity important?

Because it allows us to live out

- Our dignity as persons to the full, involving the physical-psychological-emotional qualities, spirit and body, in an overall project of life: two in one, one heart and one soul, one communion of life and love
- Our sexuality lived within conjugal love, understood as the joyful and mutual communion of all that one has and is, as a disinterested, total, and definitive gift of oneself to the other: the complete opposite

of an eroticism characterized as consumption and commerce

- Self-mastery as a virtue: "Self-mastery is a *long and exacting work*. One can never consider it acquired once and for all. It presupposes renewed effort at all stages of life. The effort required can be more intense in certain periods, such as when the personality is being formed during childhood and adolescence" (CCC, no. 2342).
- Waiting as a valuable time for growth and the realization of true love
- Our relationship with our own bodies in their complete human and Christian significance
- Pure and true friendship with our neighbor as spiritual communion

What are the characteristics of chastity?

✠ It must be observed in both marriage and virginity (i.e., in all states of life).

✠ "Chastity has laws of growth which progress through stages marked by imperfection and too often by sin. 'Man . . . day by day builds himself up through his many free decisions; and so he knows, loves, and accomplishes moral good by stages of growth'" (CCC, no. 2343).

✠ It requires a gradual and complete formation of the will, the sentiments, the emotions.

✠ "Chastity leads him who practices it to become a witness to his neighbor of God's fidelity and loving kindness . . . It shows the disciple how to follow and imitate him who has chosen us as his friends, who has given himself totally to us and allows us to participate in his divine estate. Chastity is a promise of immortality" (CCC, nos. 2345-2346).

✠ It involves

- The integrity of the person. The chaste person preserves the integrity of the forces of life and love that are in him or her, in part through "the cardinal virtue of *temperance*, which seeks to permeate the passions and appetites of the senses with reason" (CCC, no. 2341).
- The integrity of the gift of self. The chaste person integrates sexuality into his or her personhood. Self-mastery is ordered to the gift of self, it is a school of the gift of the person.

✠ It protects sexuality from being manipulated and trivialized, and rediscovers it as a divine mystery, an encounter with the other, which is a proclamation of the encounter with God.

✠ It prevents

- The reduction of the person to a mere instrument, to be possessed as if the person were an object
- Falling into individualistic, egotistical interests
- The production of bitter fruits of exploitation and violence

✠ Chastity is therefore *not*

- A rejection of sexuality
- A disdain of the values and demands of sexuality

Is everyone called to live chastity?

✠ Every person is called to chastity, according to his or her state in life. The demands of this virtue are imposed on all: on the young, on married couples, on the single, on consecrated persons.

✠ The ways in which chastity is exercised vary, of course, according to one's state in life: sexual and acceptable genital acts are morally good only within marriage, in which their exercise is nonetheless regulated by this same virtue of chastity.

✠ "Individuals should be endowed with [chastity] according to their state of life: for some it will mean virginity or celibacy consecrated to God, which is an eminent way of giving oneself more easily to God alone with an undivided heart. For others it will take the form determined by the moral law, according to whether they are married or single" (*Persona Humana*, no. 11). Married people are called to live conjugal chastity; others practice chastity in continence.

✠ "Those who are engaged to marry are called to live chastity in continence. They should see in this time of testing a discovery of mutual respect, an apprenticeship in fidelity, and the hope of receiving one another from God. They should reserve for marriage the expressions of affection that belong to married love. They will help each other grow in chastity" (CCC, nos. 2349-2350).

✠ The Christian tradition has always affirmed the value of virginity and of celibacy, which promote relationships of chaste friendship among persons, and at the same time are a sign of the eschatological realization of all created love in the uncreated love of the Blessed Trinity.

Is it easy to live chastity?

Faithfulness to the demands of a chaste life can be difficult and can require sacrifices. But difficult does not mean impossible. Chastity is the fruit of

- God's grace. "It is also a gift from God, a grace, a fruit of spiritual effort. The Holy Spirit enables one whom the water of Baptism has regenerated to imitate the purity of Christ" (CCC, no. 2345).
- A personal commitment. Those who turn with trust to prayer and the sacraments can fight victoriously against temptations, and the victories they win are a source of spiritual joy.
- The cultural effort that all of society must bring into play. It is true that, in our eroticized civilization, many alluring voices insinuate that resisting impulses considered irresistible can cause psychological disturbances. But this means a failure to see how much the person can grow by accepting responsibility courageously and mastering his or her instinctive impulses.

Philosophical reason already intuits this; and then, in the light of faith, this fight for freedom takes on a new dimension.

How are people formed to become chaste?

✠ Formation in chastity involves

- A commitment to education in sexuality that begins at the earliest age, through the parents first and then through teachers, supporting the growth of the person with personalized dialogue. The example is prayer. Sexual information and education
  - Must always be situated in the context of learning to love and live chastely
  - Must always be positive and prudent, clear and delicate
  - Are the right and duty of every parent. The school or educational institution has a supporting role in cooperation with them.
- The offering of courses in chaste living, love, and human affection to parents, educators, and children. The Catholic Church maintains that sexual education and formation in chaste living, a fundamental right and duty of the parents, must always be carried out under their watchful guidance, both at home and in the educational institutions chosen and monitored by them. In this sense, the Church reiterates the law of subsidiarity, which the school is required to observe when it cooperates in sexual and chastity

education, putting itself into the same frame of mind as the parents.

- Respect for the rights of the person, in particular that of receiving information and education that respect the moral and spiritual dimensions of human life

- A correct stewardship of sexuality, in regard to affectivity, love, and sexuality, in order to see how, in a perspective of faith, this "world of passions" can be reconciled and lived out in a mature manner by men and women

- An aid to young people in such a way that they may succeed in finding answers, discovering the reasons for and the joy of accepting a certain way of life in chastity

- An "education of the senses" that is neither an unconditional assent to them nor synonymous with mortification or privation but rather an attempt to bring out the best of one's own body, through a certain discipline and self-control: a critical, intellectual, intentional control made possible by one's scale of values

- *Purity of thought, intention, and the eyes*, through the discipline of the sentiments and the imagination, and through the rejection of any complacency in impure thoughts

- Education in *all of the other human and Christian virtues*, and in a particular way in *Christian love*, which is characterized by respect, altruism, and service, and is definitively referred to as *charity*

- The rejection of the "exaltation of the body" typical of "secular morality," with which adolescents and young people must come to terms, inundated by false and destructive messages and images of a young, beautiful, desirable body that does not age, ready to be "enjoyed" in the most varied of ways, which can be constantly renewed at the gym, the beauty salon, with plastic surgery

- A purification of the social environment, liberating it from its widespread eroticism, its morbid curiosity, its moral permissiveness. In particular, there is a vital need to protect youth and all individuals and families from the evil and dangers of pornography, particularly widespread on the Internet and the cause of damaging addiction.

✠ In the resolution of the European Parliament on so-called "sexual and reproductive health and rights" (approved on July 3, 2002), there are (together with negative or questionable statements) some positive statements, such as the need for sexual education to be proposed in a differentiated manner (art. 16), according to the age and different sexual structure of girls and boys, and the "holistic and positive way that pays attention to the psycho-social as well as bio-medical aspects and is based on mutual respect and responsibility" (art. 17).

✠ In particular, there is the need for education and formation in modesty.

Why is modesty necessary?

✠ "Purity requires *modesty*, an integral part of temperance. Modesty protects the intimate center of the person. It means refusing to unveil what should remain hidden. It is ordered to chastity to whose sensitivity it bears witness. It guides how one looks at others and behaves toward them in conformity with the dignity of persons and their solidarity.

✠ "Modesty protects the mystery of persons and their love. It encourages patience and moderation in loving relationships; it requires that the conditions for the definitive giving and commitment of man and woman to one another be fulfilled. Modesty is decency. It inspires one's choice of clothing. It keeps silence or reserve where there is evident risk of unhealthy curiosity. It is discreet.

✠ "There is a modesty of the feelings as well as of the body. It protests, for example, against the voyeuristic explorations of the human body in certain advertisements, or against the solicitations of certain media that go too far in the exhibition of intimate things. Modesty inspires a way of life which makes it possible to resist the allurements of fashion and the pressures of prevailing ideologies.

✠ "The forms taken by modesty vary from one culture to another. Everywhere, however, modesty exists as an intuition of the spiritual dignity proper to man. It is born with the awakening consciousness of being a subject. Teaching modesty to children and adolescents means awakening in them respect for the human person" (CCC, nos. 2521-2554).

✠ Modesty involves respect for *privacy*: if children or young people see that their just privacy is respected, they learn that they are expected to demonstrate the same attitude toward others. In this way, they learn to cultivate their own sense of responsibility before God, developing their inner life and their appreciation of individual freedom, which makes them capable of loving God and others better.

✠ Why should the intimate parts of one's body not be exposed for others to see? For various complementary reasons:

- Out of respect for one's own right to privacy
- In order to make a gift of one's sexual intimacy only to the person with whom one has decided to share, forever, all of oneself in marriage: heart, mind, soul, body
- Out of respect for the common sense of modesty prevailing in a particular culture or place
- In order to protect minors in particular, and those who might be offended by a certain way of dressing
- To avoid creating, for one's neighbor, any situations of embarrassment or occasions of sin

✠

For more on this topic, see the following pontifical documents:

Catechism of the Catholic Church, nos. 2231-2400
Compendium of the CCC, nos. 487-502
Congregation for the Doctrine of the Faith, *Persona Humana*, 1975

International Theological Commission, *Communion and Stewardship: Human Persons Created in the Image of God*, nos. 32-39, 2004

Pontifical Council for the Family, *The Truth and Meaning of Human Sexuality*, 1995

XI
Premarital Sex

Should engaged couples have sexual relations?

Two premises:

✠ The answer to this question depends on the value and significance that is attributed to the sexual act, properly understood as the conjugal act. In this section, I express the value of sexuality with a dimension that I call "personalistic."

✠ What is meant here is a serious relationship between "boyfriend" and "girlfriend," in the perspective of an eventual marriage. Therefore in this section we will not consider "casual sexual relations with whomever," but only the intimate relationship between a man and a woman who are seriously committed to their journey toward marriage.

When does the sexual relationship realize the fullness of its value and significance?

When it realizes the personalistic dimension, which is present when the sexual relationship between a man and a woman

- Expresses a certain kind of love for one another: disinterested, total, faithful, and indissoluble (unitive significance). Precisely because the sexual relationship involves all of the dimensions of the person (physical, psychological, affective, spiritual . . . body and soul in their dual unity), it also involves all of these characteristics of love.

    In order for the sexual act to be authentic and complete its value and significance, the man and the woman must recognize and welcome one another as gift, belonging, an integral and definitive communion of life and love (see the section "Human Sexuality").

- Respects openness to life (procreative significance), which it (the sexual act) possesses by nature. And therefore any contraceptive action must be avoided (see the section "Parenthood").

- Is realized in a context of free choice and shared psychological and affective maturity

- Takes place in a stable and definitive state of life, which is officially accepted and recognized by
    - The civil community, with civil marriage (it should not be forgotten that marriage and the family are the fundamental and central cell of society, a fundamental element of the common good of every society, an extraordinary and decisive resource for social cohesion, the true pillar of the future of humanity)

- The religious community: for the Christian, in the Sacrament of Matrimony, or in a valid, natural marriage (see the section "Marriage and Family")

On what is this personalistic dimension based?

It is based on three complementary pillars:

✠ On human experience: there are some persons who in the past have lived out this personalistic dimension of the sexual act, who are living it out in the present, who are committed to living it out in the future. Are there many of these people, or few of them? It doesn't matter very much. The fact that someone has lived out or is living out such an experience demonstrates that it is also possible for others to live it out.

✠ On rational reflection on

- The nature and dignity of the human person (see the section "In the Image of God")
- A positive view of human sexuality (see the section "Human Sexuality")

✠ On the Christian faith, which purifies, illuminates, and completes rational reflection (see the section "Science")

Under what conditions is it possible to realize concretely this personalistic dimension?

✠ Under certain indispensable and complementary conditions. Particularly indispensable are

- A serious and positive education in love, which has its origin and center in the family environment
- A harmonious overall development of the person toward psychological maturation, in view of his or her full affective and spiritual maturity
- A free and deliberate acceptance of one's responsibilities
- The development of certain gifts: mastery and gift of self (a gift is not a loan); respect and acceptance of the other for what he or she is, more than for what he or she has or gives
- A serious journey of growth in order to transform the sexual instinct into responsible desire, and this into true love
- A harmonious integration between "human values" and the "Christian content" of marriage
- A rediscovery of the value and virtue of chastity

✠ Also fundamental for the Christian is a deliberate use of the various forms of help that are offered by the Christian faith; and moreover the trusting recourse, in the face of one's errors and sins, to repentance and the merciful love of God the Father.

What effects stem from this personalistic conception of the sexual act?

✠ It must be stressed first of all that this personalistic vision emerges from a very positive, beautiful, grand, elevated conception of sexuality.

It is in the first place and above all a "yes" to this way of considering sex and the person.

And therefore the "no" that the personalistic dimension says to pre-marital relations does not emerge

- From a negative view of sexuality (prohibitionism)
- From a rejection of it
- From fear of it (erotophobia)

✠ It realizes certain important values and objectives, such as

- Respecting the dignity and integrity of the person. When the person instead seeks only or primarily pleasure in the sexual act, he or she reduces himself or herself and the other (even if unintentionally or with the other's consent) to an object, thing, instrument, possession, something disposable, contradicting the dignity of the person and of sexuality itself, which is not something to be consumed or a source of gratification for its own sake.
- Avoiding the trivialization of the sexual act, which takes place when it is reduced to the physical and sensual dimension alone, basing it completely on the genitalia and emptying it of its most authentic and complete significance, which is precisely "that of expressing and actualizing a communion of total, definitive, and publicly recognized love, which can be had only with marriage and must be built through long and patient practice" (Italian Episcopal Conference, *Evangelization and the Sacrament of Marriage*, no. 77)

- Avoiding any form of pressure, blackmail, or violence, respecting the pace and willingness of the other
- Permitting one to remain chaste, to preserve integrity in order to make a unique and exclusive gift of self to the one who will be chosen and received one day as spouse
- Encouraging an approach to the time of engagement as a long and painstaking journey; as an opportunity for the couple to verify and explore each other's human and Christian maturity; as a privileged moment of grace, of growth in the faith, of prayer and participation in the liturgical life of the Church, of an experience lived in Christian charity
- Preparing that total and fecund love that is typical of conjugal life. Being able to wait and avoiding sexual relations helps the engaged couple to grow "in mutual understanding and in the assimilation of one another's personality; it guides them in the development of a dedicated and profound affectivity; it makes them capable of mastering their selfish instincts, in respect for personal dignity; gift of self for the future, because it is only in marriage that it reaches the fullness of its significance" (*Evangelization and the Sacrament of Marriage*, no. 76).
- Allowing the couple to concentrate, with the calm and seriousness necessary, on the issues that will be a normal part of their married life: from the psychological issues in their relationship as a couple to the legal issues of joint or separate ownership of assets

and the rights and duties of married life; from the medical-biological issues related to their sexual relationship and the transmission of life to those concerning responsible fatherhood and motherhood and knowledge of the natural methods for regulating fertility; from those concerning the dignity and beauty of Christian marriage and family to those concerning the right way to raise children and the orderly conduct of the family (stable work, sufficient financial resources, wise administration, notions of household management . . .) (see *Familiaris Consortio*, no. 66)

■ Also respecting Christian sexual morality, avoiding the commission of sexual sins in thought, word, and action. In fact, for the baptized, premarital relations "constitute the disordered use of a human sexuality that the Savior has situated in reference to his own love and his kingdom." They are not and cannot be a true sign of that new love that Jesus gives to the spouses with the Sacrament of Matrimony; they are, instead, a counterfeit of it (see *Persona Humana*, no. 7).

What response should be given to those who object: "If two people care about each other, why shouldn't they express it in the sexual act?"

Here is how to respond:

✠ It must be clarified immediately what is meant by *caring about each other*. There are in fact various levels and ways of actualizing this care.

If one means

- *Caring about each other* as it is understood in the personalistic approach, and that is as a self-donation that is total, definitive, exclusive, sanctioned officially (socially) and for the Christian also sacramentally; and therefore a *caring about each other* that realizes a giving and receiving of all of oneself and forever; a wanting to say to the other: *I am ready to give my life for you, now and forever* . . .
- And the sexual act as a way of expressing this type and level of *caring about each other,*
- Then it is understandable how *caring about each other* is truly something great, and the sexual act is fully justified if and when it expresses all of this, which it can only do in marriage as the union of one man and one woman. If it does not express all of this, the sexual act remains incomplete and "premature" (*Persona Humana,* no. 7). In a certain sense it is a lie, even if it is complete from a physical-physiological point of view, and even if it is in a sense "rewarding" in psychological terms.

✠ It is also necessary to keep in mind that performing a sexual act without this kind of *caring about each other* can easily lead people into error. In fact:

- The intense psychological pleasure that is sometimes felt can lead someone to think erroneously that there is a perfect and total understanding between the two persons involved, ignoring or minimizing the differences that exist on the other essential levels of understanding and relation (character, interests, ideals, hierarchy of values, configuration and vision of life, both personal and conjugal-familial, having and raising children . . .), thereby exempting the persons involved from seeking a dialogue-verification-encounter-understanding on these levels.

- But if on the contrary the sexual act should involve a sense of disappointment, sadness, bitterness, all of this could lead a couple to think that they are not made for each other, that they are incompatible, not suited for married life . . . when instead it may be simply a question of jumping the gun, of a lack of understanding, of an absence of true and full caring about each other . . . elements that, if present, would certainly lead to better sexual compatibility as well.

In what sense does the premarital sexual act constitute

✠ A theft with regard to the person?

The person who performs a premarital sexual act deprives himself or herself and the other partner (present or future) of the right to priority and exclusivity in giving and receiving the gift of one's self in the sexual act, in the fullness of its value and significance (for the Christian, this includes divine, sacramental blessing and sanctification). In this way, both of the persons are victims of a serious theft, being defrauded of these essential aspects of their sexual dimension.

How wonderful, right, and dutiful it would be, and at the same time gratifying and rewarding, to be able to make a gift of one's first sexual act to the other whom one loves completely and marries forever!

✠ An obstacle to true and full understanding of the other? The premarital sexual act

- Obstructs true and full mutual understanding, inducing the illusion of knowing each other deeply, because a sufficient or even a good sexual understanding has been reached
- Leads to an under-appreciation of the fact that sexual harmony of the couple depends, in reality, above all on the quality of love, on the capacity to be gift with and for the other, and not mainly from a physical and sexual rapport
- Detracts from the pursuit of other values of engagement, and also from other ways of expressing tenderness and communication as a couple
- Does not help in the construction of healthy relationships, but rather encourages superficiality

✠ A limitation on one's own freedom and that of others?
The premarital act implies a certain commitment between the two partners. Now experience teaches that

- Wherever there have been sexual relations, it becomes more difficult to call into question one's decision or break off the relationship. One might be less free in establishing a new, definitive, and positive relationship, all the more so as the moment of the "fateful yes" of the wedding day approaches.

- The sexual relationship sometimes takes place in an absence of freedom, or even as a form of real and proper blackmail. By not "giving in," one fears being rejected by one's partner ("if I don't do it, he/she will leave me").
- Sexual relations
  - Sometimes give rise to the demand to live together, sharply accelerating or sidestepping the other indispensable stages that are required by "living together well"
  - Other times delay the decision to marry, making the sexual rapport seem rewarding and sufficient
- Moreover, when one has been "burned and jaded," disappointed by one or more sexual relationships, this can have psychological and emotional consequences that make the next sexual relationship very difficult
- If to all of this is added the possibility of pregnancy, unplanned and often unwanted in these premarital situations . . . it can be understood how one's own freedom and that of the other (not only of the other spouse, but also and above all of the defenseless unborn child, in particular in the case of the grave temptation of abortion) is gravely undermined and limited

Doesn't the premarital relationship represent a true "experiment" in marriage?

No, because married life is much different from the engagement period. Living together is not a trial of marriage, because it takes place outside of the decision that involves exclusivity, definitive stability, lifelong responsibility for another's life, without the possibility of return and in a state of life that is recognized and accepted by the civil community and often by the religious community as well. These are realities for which only marriage is binding.

Experience also teaches that even more or less extended periods of cohabitation have not always led to the decision to marry or to true and lasting marriages.

What concluding points can be drawn from what is presented above?

I draw two conclusions:

✠ It has not been demonstrated that premarital sexual relations constitute a real preparation, a positive education for marriage. On the contrary, in the light of the personalistic dimension described above, they are anti-marital, in that they defraud, they impoverish, sometimes they even impede or destroy it.

✠ The reasons presented above in support of this affirmation, which are rooted in the personalistic dimension of the sexual relationship, can also be understood well and shared by non-Christians, in that, as has been seen, they do not primarily enlist arguments and reasoning derived from the Christian faith. Therefore a non-Christian can also understand them perfectly and even share them. All that is needed is a good use of one's rational faculties.

✠

For more on this topic, see the following documents:

>*Catechism of the Catholic Church*, nos. 2331-2400
>*Compendium of the* CCC, nos. 487-502
>Congregation for the Doctrine of the Faith, *Persona Humana*, 1975
>International Theological Commission, *Communion and Stewardship: Human Persons Created in the Image of God*, 2004, nos. 32-39
>Pontifical Council for the Family, *The Truth and Meaning of Human Sexuality*, 1995
>Italian Episcopal Conference, *Direttorio di Pastorale familiare per la Chiesa in Italia*

XII
Homosexuality

According to Christian morality, what is the difference, in homosexuality, between inclination and act?

✠ A homosexual tendency or inclination (same-sex attraction), although it is objectively disordered, must not be considered sinful in itself. As the *Catechism* teaches, "its psychological genesis remains largely unexplained," and "the number of men and women who have deep-seated homosexual tendencies is not negligible. This inclination, which is objectively disordered, constitutes for most of them a trial" (CCC, nos. 2357, 2358).

✠ The homosexual inclination is disordered in the sense that it is not ordered or aligned to the true good of the person and thus can lead to disordered and sinful acts. This is not to say that the person is disordered; rather it is the inclination that is misaligned, or at cross-purposes with oneself, and therefore calls for proper pastoral, spiritual, and psychological attention.

✠ The homosexual act, however, is a sin gravely contrary to chastity. In fact, it excludes the gift of life. It is not the fruit of a true affective and sexual complementarity. In no way can it be approved.

✠ Homosexual acts "are expressions of the vice of lust. These kinds of acts committed against the physical and moral integrity of minors become even more grave" (*Compendium of the* CCC, no. 492).

What attitude does the Church require in regard to homosexual behavior?

✠ The Church says "yes" to

- The intrinsic dignity of all persons, including persons who experience same-sex attraction. Every person, precisely as a person, is owed dignity, acceptance, and help. One cannot forget, in fact, that every human person, male and female, is created in the image of God.
- The decriminalization of homosexuality in the state legal system, while also not seeking to promote, protect, or privilege homosexual behavior
- The distinction
  - Between sinner and sin
  - Between a crime (legal aspect) and sin (moral aspect)
  - Between the homosexual inclination and homosexual acts

- Respect for the specific and basic human rights of individual persons, rights that persons who experience same-sex attraction also have as persons and as citizens, no more or less than other human persons, and not on the basis of experiencing a homosexual inclination
- The education and formation in chastity, and, where possible, the healing of persons who experience same-sex attraction
- The creation of concrete pastoral initiatives on behalf of persons who experience same-sex attraction
- Calling all persons to chastity and holiness
- Prayer and sacramental life, as light and help for the person with a homosexual inclination to live in chastity

✠ The Church says "no" to

- Approval of homosexual behavior or homosexual relationships
- The conception of homosexuality as a dimension completely beyond or above moral norms
- Legally recognizing and privileging the homosexual relationship or equating it with marriage
- Permitting same-sex "couples" to be foster or adoptive parents. Every child has a mother and a father, and every child has a basic right to be known and raised by his or her mother and father together in an intact home. The child needs a father and a mother for

healthy human maturation, for a correct view of the family and a secure sense of his or her place in life.

- Every instance of unjust discrimination, to every form of rejection, marginalization, or disdain toward persons who experience same-sex attraction

Can persons with a homosexual inclination become priests?

✠ Holy Orders cannot be granted to those who

- Perform homosexual acts (within the last three years before priestly ordination)
- Present deeply rooted homosexual tendencies
- Support the "gay culture"

✠ Those who have homosexual tendencies of a transitory nature can be admitted to Holy Orders, as long as these tendencies have been clearly overcome at least three years before ordination to the diaconate (see Congregation for Catholic Education, *Instruction Concerning the Criteria for the Discernment of Vocations with Regard to Persons with Homosexual Tendencies in View of Their Admission to the Seminary and to Holy Orders*, November 4, 2005).

Are there similar fruits produced by conjugal love and relations between two persons of the same sex?

✠ The love between man and woman has the power to generate various and complementary "loves": conjugal, parental, fraternal, and filial.

A same-sex relationship does not have this broadness of life. It exhausts itself in the relationship between two persons.

✠ The richness of life that the conjugal relationship produces in persons and the benefits that it gives to society, particularly in its essential contribution to the common good, are unique and cannot in any way be equated with a relationship between two persons of the same sex.

Can an analogy be established between marriage and homosexual relationships?

There is no foundation whatsoever for assimilating or establishing analogies, even remote ones, between homosexual relationships and God's plan for marriage and the family. Marriage is holy, while homosexual relations are contrary to the natural moral order. In Sacred Scripture, homosexual relations are condemned as grave depravities (see Rom 1:24-27; 1 Cor 6:10; 1 Tm 1:10).

Why shouldn't homosexual relationships be legally recognized and privileged?

For various and complementary reasons:

✠ The natural reason: Civil law cannot enter into contradiction with right reason without losing its power to bind the conscience. Every law made by human beings has the force of law only insofar as it is in keeping with the natural moral law, recognized by right reason, and insofar as it respects in particular the inalienable rights of every person. Legislation in favor of homosexual relationships is contrary to right reason, because it confers on the relationship between two persons of the same sex legal guarantees analogous to those for the institution of marriage.

✠ The biological-anthropological reason: Homosexual relationships are completely lacking in those biological and anthropological elements that are proper to marriage and the family.

In fact, a same-sex relationship

- Lacks sexual difference and the genital-sexual differentiation that is the objective attribute with which we come into the world: male or female. This original attribute is inscribed in the body, the mind, the soul.
- Completely lacks the conjugal dimension, which represents the properly ordered and human form of sexual relations. These, in fact, are human when and to the extent that they express and promote the mutual help of the two sexes in marriage.
- Does not accomplish procreation and the survival of the human species
- Because of the absence of sexual difference, complementarity, and reciprocity, creates obstacles for the normal development of any children brought into these homosexual relationships. These children lack the experience of motherhood or fatherhood. Bringing children into the environment of homosexual relationships through adoption is a form of violence against these children, in the sense that their weakness is exploited in order

to bring them into environments that do not foster their full human development. Such a practice would certainly be gravely immoral and would be in open contradiction with the principle, recognized also by the United Nations Convention on the Rights of the Child, according to which the highest interest to be protected in every case is that of the child, the weakest and most defenseless party.

✠ The social reason:

- Legally recognizing homosexual relationships means
  - Approving of a deviant behavior
  - Making it a model for society
  - Approving of sexual indeterminacy
  - Obfuscating the fundamental values and personal/social coordinates of marriage and the family. In fact, the concept of marriage would undergo a radical change, with grave detriment to the common good. It would lose its essential reference to the factors connected to sexual difference, such as the tasks of procreation and child raising.
- There are also good reasons to say that homosexual relations are harmful to the proper development of human society, above all if their actual impact on the social fabric were increased.
- At the foundation of human history are not two sexually undifferentiated individuals, but a couple: a man and a woman, a community-communion of two

persons who complement one another and, open to new life, generate the community: community from community.

- There is also the danger that legislation making homosexuality a basis for claiming rights could in fact encourage a person with homosexual tendencies to declare his or her homosexuality and even seek a "partner" for the purpose of exploiting the provisions of the law.

✠ The legal reason: Since married couples play the role of guaranteeing the continuation of the generations and are therefore eminently in the public interest, civil law confers institutional recognition on them. Homosexual relationships, on the other hand, do not require special attention on the part of the legal system, because they do not play the aforementioned role for the common good. Persons who experience same-sex attraction, as persons and as citizens, can always resort—as can all citizens on the basis of their private autonomy—to the universally applicable law in order to resolve legal situations of mutual interest.

What does the Catholic Church ask the state to do in regard to homosexual relationships?

✠ The Catholic Church asks the state to

- Clearly affirm the immoral nature of this kind of union
- Contain the phenomenon within limits that do not endanger the fabric of public morality

- Recall that the tolerance of evil is something very different from the approval or legalization of evil
- Unmask the instrumental or ideological use that can be made of the proper tolerance of persons who experience same-sex attraction
- Not proceed with the legal recognition of homosexual relationships or with equating them legally with marriage, with access to the rights that are proper to the latter, as such would constitute the unjust and intrinsically evil redefinition of marriage in the law
- Respect the principle of equality, by virtue of which the same benefits and advantages cannot and should not be attributed to persons who are not and cannot be in the same legal situation. In fact, while persons bound by marriage are required to observe a number of duties and obligations stipulated by family law, persons in de facto unions can exempt themselves from these obligations at will. Thus the state would violate the principle of equality by conferring on persons in de facto unions the benefits that the law justly provides only for conjugal family unions. Further, to treat different things differently is not unjust discrimination.

✠ The common commitment of the state and of the Church, although on different levels and by different means, is above all that of not exposing the younger generations to an erroneous conception of sexuality and marriage, which would deprive them of the necessary defenses and would also contribute to the spread of the phenomenon itself.

Some say: The legal recognition of homosexual relationships would not oblige anyone to make use of these laws. So why not provide for those who would like to make use of them?

✠ In this regard, one must reflect on the difference between homosexual behavior as a private phenomenon and the same behavior as a legally established and approved social relationship, to the point of becoming one of the institutions of the legal system. The latter phenomenon is not only graver, but it takes on a much more vast and profound significance, and would end up making changes to the entire social organization that would be contrary to the common good.

✠ Civil law is a structuring principle of human life in society, for good or for ill. It plays a very important role in promoting a mentality and customs. The forms of life and the models expressed in it not only give social life its contours but also tend to change how the new generations understand and evaluate behaviors. The legal recognition of homosexual relationships would thus be destined to cause an obscuring of the perception of certain fundamental moral values and the devaluing, erosion, and redefinition of the institution of marriage.

What must Catholic politicians do with regard to legislation in favor of homosexual relationships?

✠ If a bill in favor of the legal recognition of homosexual relationships (whether as civil unions, domestic partnerships, etc.) were proposed in the legislative assembly for the first time, the Catholic politician would have the moral duty to express his or her disagreement clearly and publicly, and vote against the bill. Voting for a bill so harmful for the common good would be a gravely immoral act.

✠ If a law in favor of homosexual "unions" were already in force, he or she must oppose it as far as possible, and make this opposition known. If it were not possible to abrogate completely a law of this kind, he or she could licitly offer support to proposals aimed at limiting the damage of such a law and diminishing its negative effects on the level of culture and public morality, on the condition that his or her absolute personal opposition to such laws be clear and known to all, and that the danger of scandal be avoided.

For more on this topic, see the following documents:

Congregation for the Doctrine of the Faith, *Considerations Regarding Proposals to Give Legal Recognition to Unions Between Homosexual Persons*, June 3, 2003; *Persona Humana*, December 29, 1975, no. 8; *Letter to the Bishops of the Catholic Church on the Pastoral Care of Homosexual Persons*, October 1, 1986; *Some Considerations Concerning the Response to Legislative*

Proposals on the Non-discrimination of Homosexual Persons, July 24, 1992

Catechism of the Catholic Church, nos. 2357-2359, 2396

Congregation for Catholic Education, *Instruction Concerning the Criteria for the Discernment of Vocations with Regard to Persons with Homosexual Tendencies in View of Their Admission to the Seminary and to Holy Orders*, November 4, 2005.

XIII
Marriage and Family

What is marriage?

It is that special communion of life and love between a man and a woman, in which specific characteristics and purposes are realized.

What are the characteristics and purposes of marriage?

✠ They are various and complementary:

- The mutual personal donation that is proper and exclusive to husband and wife
- Heterosexuality, or sexual difference, which leads to interpersonal complementarity
- Unity
- Faithfulness

- Indissolubility
- Fecundity, or fruitfulness
- The good of the spouses (mutual help, respect, harmony, assistance . . .)
- Child raising
- Openness and commitment to the Christian and social community

✠ These characteristics and purposes are significant even on the human level, and all the more so in Christian life, in which marriage is a sacrament.

What relationship is established between man and woman in marriage?

Man and woman are equal as persons and complementary as male and female. In this way they perfect one another. Their spousal union includes the sexual dimension, in which body and spirit unite, "so they are no longer two, but one flesh" (Mt 19:6), and at the same time they collaborate with God in generating and forming new human lives.

Marital union, according to the original divine plan, is indissoluble: "What God has joined together, no human being must separate" (Mt 19:6).

On what is this conception based?

This conception of marriage

- Is the will of God the Creator, who, at the beginning of the world, created man "male and female" (Gn 1:27)

- Is demonstrated by right reason
- Is recognized as such by all the major religions
- Has been elevated by Christ to the dignity of a sacrament (between a baptized man and a baptized woman)
- Has as its model the Holy Family of Nazareth, which is the prototype and exemplar of all Christian families

What is the relationship between marriage and family?

The family is the natural society founded on marriage as the union of a man and a woman. Therefore a man and a woman, united in marriage, together with their children, constitute a family. Each of them is a person equal in dignity to the others, although each has his or her proper and complementary responsibilities.

On what are marriage and the family founded?

"Marriage and the family are not in fact a chance sociological construction, the product of particular historical and financial situations. On the other hand, the question of the right relationship between the man and the woman is rooted in the essential core of the human being and it is only by starting from here that its response can be found . . . Marriage as an institution is thus not an undue interference of society or of authority. The external imposition of form on the most private reality of life is instead an intrinsic requirement of the covenant of conjugal love and of the depths of the human person" (Pope Benedict XVI, Address to the participants in the Ecclesial Diocesan Convention of Rome, June 6, 2006).

What is the role of the family?

✠ On the social level, it is

- A natural institution, characterized by an unrepeatable and irreplaceable uniqueness
- The fundamental and central cell of society, existing before the state; a fundamental element of the common good of every society; an extraordinary and decisive resource for social cohesion; a true pillar of the future of society; the intermediary cell between the individual and the state, and between intermediate societies and the state
- The first and essential level of social articulation
- The first natural society, "a divine institution that stands at the foundation of life of the human person as the prototype of every social order" (*Compendium of the Social Doctrine of the Church*, no. 211)
- The primary place of the humanization of the person and of society
- The source and the primary resource of society and solidarity
- The fundamental experience of communion and human and social responsibility
- The environment of the social advancement of the person
- The bearer of historical, social, and economic values

✠ On the level of the person, the family is

- The environment of the communion of life and love of the person
- The cradle of life and love
- The natural place of the transmission and continuity of life, of growth, and of the protection of the person
- The hearth at which human life is born and is welcomed generously and responsibly; the environment in which the person is educated for life, and in which the parents, loving their children with tenderness, prepare them to establish healthy interpersonal relationships that embody the moral and human values
- The bearer of original rights, significantly recognized, in general, at the civil level as well
- The school of human and Christian virtues; the training ground of human and civil values
- The community of faith, hope, and charity
- The place of the first proclamation and of the growth and testimony of the Christian faith
- The domestic Church, sanctuary of the life and Christian growth of the person. It is therefore called to live and witness to the Gospel of love, so as to present and explain the beauty of the Gospel teaching on love.

✠ "The Holy See sought to acknowledge a special juridic dignity proper to the family by publishing the Charter of the Rights of the Family. In its Preamble we read: 'The rights of the person, even if they are expressed as rights of the individual, have a fundamental social dimension which finds an innate and vital expression in the family.' The rights set forth in the Charter are an expression and explicitation of the natural law written on the heart of the human being and made known to him by reason. The denial or even the restriction of the rights of the family, by obscuring the truth about man, threatens the very foundations of peace" (Pope Benedict XVI, Message for the celebration of the World Day of Peace, January 1, 2008).

What does it mean that marriage is a sacrament?

✠ It means that marriage

- Has its roots in the heart of God the Creator (see Gn 2:24)
- Expresses the love that circulates among the Persons of the Trinity and the fecundity of their relationship (see *Dignitatis Personae*, no. 9)
- Is an efficacious sign of the covenant between Christ and the Church (see Eph 5:32), which means that it manifests and embodies the spousal love of Christ for the Church. "Husbands, love your wives, even as Christ loved the church" (Eph 5:25), giving his life for it.

✠ This Christian significance does not diminish, but confirms and reinforces the human value of marriage. "The family finds in the plan of God the Creator and Redeemer not only its identity, what it is, but also its mission, what it can and should do. The role that God calls the family to perform in history derives from what the family is; its role represents the dynamic and existential development of what it is. Each family finds within itself a summons that cannot be ignored, and that specifies both its dignity and its responsibility: family, become what you are" (*Familiaris Consortio*, no. 17).

Why is conjugal love indissoluble?

The reasons for the indissolubility of conjugal love are

- The very nature of conjugal love, which is total and faithful
- The original plan of God
- The good of the children
- Its being a "sacramental sign" of the indissoluble love of Christ for the Church

What is the significance of the conjugal sexual act?

It has a twofold significance: unitive (the complementary donation of love, total and definitive, of husband and wife) and procreative (openness to the procreation of a new life and fruitfulness).

Is it moral to prevent procreation?

✠ Every marital act must remain open, in itself, to the transmission of life. Any action is therefore intrinsically immoral which, in view of or in the performance or development of the natural consequences of the conjugal relationship, should propose, as an end or a means, to make procreation impossible.

✠ Contraception

- Is gravely opposed to marital chastity
- Is contrary to the good of the transmission of life (the procreative aspect of marriage) and to the mutual donation of the spouses (the unitive aspect of marriage)
- Injures true love and denies the sovereign role of God in the transmission of human life

How can the spouses regulate their fertility morally?

With periodic continence and recourse to the woman's infertile times. The testimony of couples who for years have been living in harmony with the plan of the Creator and licitly using, when there is proportionately serious reason, the methods rightly called "natural," confirms that the spouses can live in wholeness, in common accord, and with full donation the demands of chastity and conjugal life.

Why are those who have divorced and remarried not permitted to receive Holy Communion?

✠ They may not receive Holy Communion because their objective situation as divorced and remarried prevents them, since it is gravely contrary to the teaching of Christ. This is not any sort of punishment or discrimination, but only absolute fidelity to the will of Christ, who has restored the indissolubility of marriage to us as a gift of the Creator.

✠ For those who have divorced and remarried, access to Holy Communion is opened only by sacramental absolution, which can be given only to those who, repentant over having violated the teaching of Christ, are sincerely disposed to a form of life that is no longer in contradiction with the indissolubility of marriage. More specifically, this means that when the man and woman, for serious reasons—such as, for example, raising the children—are unable to satisfy the obligation of separation, they make the commitment to live in complete continence, as brother and sister, abstaining from conjugal sexual acts. In this case, they may receive Holy Communion, under the condition that they avoid giving scandal (for example, by receiving Holy Communion at a church where they are not known).

Is it easy for the spouses to meet the demands of conjugal and family life?

This is not easy, but neither is it impossible. God does not ask the impossible. Above all, to those who ask him, he gives the grace of the Holy Spirit, who, freeing the spouses from their hardness of heart, makes them capable of realizing completely, although gradually, the characteristics and purposes of conjugal and family life. Through the gift of the Holy Spirit, the spouses are made participants in Christ's capacity to love (conjugal charity).

✠ In the journey to holiness, the Christian experiences both human weakness and the kindness and mercy of the Lord. Therefore the key to the exercise of the Christian virtues, and thus also of conjugal chastity, is the ability of the faith to make us aware of God's mercy and the repentance that humbly welcomes God's forgiveness.

✠ Frequent and persevering recourse to prayer, the Eucharist, and the Sacrament of Reconciliation is therefore indispensable. The "burden" that is proper to the spouses is neither easy nor light in the sense of being small or insignificant, but it becomes light because the Lord, and with him the whole Church, shares in it.

Can marriage be equated with another kind of cohabitation?

Absolutely not. Given the nature of marriage and the family, the legitimate family must not be equated with common-law unions and other forms of non-marital cohabitation, whether homosexual or heterosexual. Above all, making these equal has no foundation in a good constitutional civil order.

What is required when one of the spouses is not Catholic?

In order to be licit, *mixed* marriages (between a Catholic and a baptized non-Catholic) require approval from the ecclesiastical authority. Those of *disparity of worship* (between a Catholic and an unbaptized person), in order to be valid, require a dispensation. In any case, it is essential that the spouses not exclude the acceptance of the essential characteristics and purposes of marriage, and that the Catholic spouse confirm with the other spouse the commitment to keeping his or her own faith and guaranteeing the Baptism and Catholic upbringing of the children.

What are the duties of society and the state in regard to the family?

✠ Society and the state have the right and the duty to

- Recognize the rights of the family and adopt every measure suitable to foster the fulfillment of the tasks assigned to them. "The family has a right to the full support of the state in order to carry out fully its particular mission" (Pope John Paul II, Message for the 27th World Day of Peace, no. 5).
- Guarantee a broader exercise of familial rights and duties, including parental responsibilities
- Foster the equal dignity of persons and the overcoming of obstacles that impede its effective realization
- Respect and promote the richness of the family as an institution of education, formation, and the transmission of values and traditions, as well as cultural and spiritual identity
- Protect children and the rights of minors and the elderly, with adequate measures of support for young couples, socially disadvantaged families, and large

families, also taking into account the real needs of spouses, the elderly, and the new generations

- Support the family in the fulfillment of its social and economic functions
- Orient to this end social, economic, and financial policies, and the organization of services
- Respect the principle of "subsidiarity," according to which the state must not take the place of the family in the fulfillment of its role and its functions, but only help and support it if necessary. In fact, the guiding principle of a true family policy is the principle of subsidiarity, which recognizes the leading role of the family, its quality as a primary resource for society, a subject to be promoted and not only to be assisted when it is in difficulty.
- Provide adequate information about access to adoption procedures

✠ The state must also, with adequate legislation, affirm, protect, and promote marriage and the family by

- Reserving for them the fundamental, unique, and exclusive place that belongs to them in society
- Not equating them with any other kind of union or cohabitation
- Avoiding the introduction in the public system of other forms of union that would contribute to destabilizing the family, obscuring its unique character and its irreplaceable social role

✠ The Universal Declaration of Human Rights itself, in particular in article 16, asserts that

- Men and women who have reached the appropriate age have the right to marry and establish a family, without any limitation of race, citizenship, or religion. They have equal rights with regard to marriage, both during marriage and in the death of one of the spouses.
- Marriage can be established only with the free and full consent of the future spouses
- The family is the natural and fundamental core of society and has the right to be protected by society and the state

✠

For more on this topic, see the following pontifical documents:

Catechism of the Catholic Church, nos. 1601-1666; 2331-2400

Compendium of the CCC, nos. 337-350; 487-502

Vatican Council II, *Gaudium et Spes*, nos. 47-50

Pontifical Council for the Family, *Charter of the Rights of the Family*, October 22, 1983

Pope Paul VI, *Humanae Vitae*, 1968

Pope John Paul II, *Familiaris Consortio*, 1982; *Mulieris Dignitatem*, 1988

Congregation for the Doctrine of the Faith, *Donum Vitae*, 1988; *Letter to the Bishops of the Catholic Church on the Collaboration of Men and Women in the Church and in the World*, 2004

XIV
Marriage Erosion

Civil Unions and Other Arrangements That Undermine Marriage

The problem:

Is it necessary, is it morally appropriate to recognize in law nonmarital sexual relationships such as found in cohabitation and de facto unions? To legally recognize them, regardless of whether the persons are of opposite sex or the same sex? To permit them to adopt? These, and other similar questions, are becoming more and more prominent in public debate.

What are the characteristics of cohabitation (understood as living together in a nonmarital sexual relationship)?

✠ With regard to sexual difference: There is heterosexual cohabitation (which reflects how the term is most commonly used) and homosexual cohabitation.

✠ With regard to the intention to marry: There are de facto couples that *do not want* to get married, those that *cannot* get married, and those that *want the legal recognition of their sexual relationship*, and not marriage.

- About the first, those that do not want to get married: The intention of the cohabitants is precisely that of—although they could do so—not binding themselves legally, and they do not see why the law should do them the "violence" of considering them bound in any case, against their will.

- About the second, the couples that cannot get married: These are divided into two subcategories.

    - The first is made up of those who cannot get married yet because of temporary impediments, generally of a legal nature (for example, because one of the persons is a minor or is waiting for a divorce, etc.). For these couples, the offer of legal recognition makes no sense; the same difficulty that precludes their marriage would also preclude legal recognition.

    - The second subcategory is composed of those couples that would like to get married but believe that they are unable to do so because of financial difficulties, and therefore delay marriage, sometimes indefinitely. The authentic way of meeting the social needs of these couples is certainly not that of offering them a "mini-marriage" (according to the incisive and ironic definition of Cardinal Ruini), which would not resolve any of the financial difficulties in question, but that of mobilizing social initiatives on behalf of the family (for example, regarding the cost of housing, child care, elder care . . .).

- About the de facto couples who want the legal recognition of their cohabitation: In this section, we will examine this kind of cohabitation in particular.

What does the Catholic Church say about cohabitation?

Above all it must be emphasized that the Church says "yes" to the person and to the family.

✠ In regard to the individual person, the Church says "yes"

- To the intrinsic and inviolable dignity of every human person. Every person is created in the image and likeness of God.
- To upholding the basic human rights of all people and to helpful legal protections for all people based on the principle of the inviolable dignity of the human person, without creating a new legal status or arrangement that erodes or redefines marriage
- To a pastoral outreach to cohabitants through concrete pastoral initiatives carried out by prepared and competent personnel

✠ In regard to the family, the Church says "yes"

- To the family founded on marriage as the union of a man and a woman. Concerning marriage, there are three distinctive and indispensable characteristics: sexual difference, permanent and exclusive fidelity between the spouses, and openness to life. And this by nature, meaning always and everywhere, and not by culture, or according to custom, ethnicity, location, or fashion. The family is not the result of a social dynamic, it is not a historical product, but a reality that comes before society and the state. The family is the fundamental and central cell of society, the first and essential level of social articulation, the origin and primary resource of society itself: "Marriage as an institution is thus not an undue interference of society or of authority. The external imposition of form on the most private reality of life is instead an intrinsic requirement of the covenant of conjugal love and of the depths of the human person" (Pope Benedict XVI, Address to the Participants in the Ecclesial Diocesan Convention of Rome).

■ To an indispensable and prioritized family policy in favor of the young; young married couples; affordable housing; poor families; the protection of childbearing, fertility, maternity; children already born and yet to be born; mothers who work in or outside of the home . . .

■ To more incisive and complete pastoral activity on behalf of the family

■ To a positive and joyful witness of married couples in the Church, so as to offer an example, an attractive model, appealing for young engaged couples and for de facto couples themselves

✠ The Church, therefore, in saying "yes" to the aforementioned fundamental realities, as a result says "no" to the legal recognition of de facto couples, which is unacceptable on the level of principle and dangerous on the social and educational level. Let's examine in detail the reasons for this "no."

Why does the Church say no to the legal recognition of nonmarital sexual relationships between a man and a woman?

Because this legal recognition

- Deprives marriage of its uniqueness, which alone justifies the rights that are proper to the spouses and belong only to them. Extending to de facto couples some of the rights previously reserved for marriage and family introduces a dangerous alternative to the family. It is unjust to claim the rights that stem from marriage without contracting it.
- Makes civil marriages worthless. If a man and a woman want the law to recognize their union, the instrument is already there, and it is a wedding at city hall.
- Has a negative influence on social mentality and customs. History teaches that every law creates mentality and custom, and this because law, any law, is in

and of itself a form of pedagogy, which induces one to think that that which is legal is also moral, and therefore has ethical ramifications.

- Makes cohabitation more convenient and accessible, even turning it into a model, an invitation, a symbol, an incentive for young people to avoid responsibility. "When new forms of legislation are created which relativize marriage, the renouncement of the definitive bond obtains, as it were, also a juridical seal. In this case, deciding for those who are already finding it far from easy becomes even more difficult" (Pope Benedict XVI, Christmas Address to the Members of the Roman Curia, December 22, 2006).

- Is in contradiction with the nature of de facto cohabitation, which contains a principle, that of the rejection of the public bond, in that preserving or dissolving the relationship depends solely on the will of the partners. This is a principle of total individualism and subjectivism, according to which the individual conscience rests on free choice alone, and can determine the relationship as a mere practical matter that is not meant to be recognized as a true public relationship.

- Conceals a fundamental error, the absolutizing principle according to which it is forbidden to forbid. Everyone is free to do as he or she believes, without the right to determine in any way the behavior of others.

- Poses some fundamental questions:

- What framework of values and principles is to be consulted concerning the conception of man, woman, the family, society, the future?
- What must be the criteria of reference in making decisions in a democratic society? Only the criterion of numerical majority?
- Who determines the actual duration and continuity of the cohabitation, and how?

■ Creates the possibility of fraud, abuse, and deceit by those who want to have rights and benefits without having any duties. In fact, how can it be verified that the sexual relationship of the cohabitants is real, and not simply declared in order to enjoy the rights that stem from legal recognition?

■ Clears the way for the legal recognition of same-sex sexual relationships, and even for the total redefinition of marriage

Why does the Church say no to the legal recognition of same-sex sexual relationships?

✠ In addition to all of the reasons given above against the legal recognition of nonmarital sexual relationships between a man and a woman, there are further reasons against the legal recognition of same-sex sexual relationships.

The Church says "no" to same-sex "unions" (and even more so to so-called same-sex "marriage"), in that they

■ Do not recognize the specific sexual difference, the objective and respective originality of each sex (woman, man); they relativize and even contradict the recognition both of the differences and of the complementarity between man and woman; they do not represent an integration of sexual complementarity. Putting a man and woman together or two persons of the same sex, therefore, becomes the same thing. There is, however, a natural structural difference inscribed in the physicality of man and woman, as well as a complementarity in view of the emotional and sexual life of the spouses.

- Cannot conceive and give life to a child, and therefore among other things cannot make that fundamental contribution to society that is procreation, that contribution without which society commits suicide. Only the family open to life can be considered the true cell of society, because it guarantees the continuity and care of the generations. The good of the generation of children is the specific reason for the social recognition of marriage. It is in the interest of society and of the state that the family be strong and grow in the most balanced way possible.

✠ Legally recognizing homosexual "unions" means

- Approving a deviant behavior
- Turning it into a model in society
- Obscuring fundamental values, such as marriage and the family
- Increasing the risk that a person with homosexual tendencies would more easily declare and embrace

his or her homosexuality as defining one's identity or even seek a "partner" for the purpose of exploiting the dispositions of the law

✠ Cardinal Joseph Ratzinger, as prefect of the CDF, stated that "the proper reaction to crimes committed against homosexual persons should not be to claim that the homosexual condition is not disordered. When such a claim is made and when homosexual activity is consequently condoned, or when civil legislation is introduced to protect behavior to which no one has any conceivable right, neither the Church nor society at large should be surprised when other distorted notions and practices gain ground, and irrational and violent reactions increase" (*Letter to the Bishops of the Catholic Church on the Pastoral Care of Homosexual Persons*, no. 10).

In what way does the legal recognition of various forms of sexual cohabitation

1. Create a grave discrimination?

✠ It creates a grave discrimination in that it treats very different situations the same. There is, in fact, a substantial difference between marriage and the various forms of sexual cohabitation, which are very different realities:

- On the objective level: There is a substantial difference between those who make a public commitment to form a nuclear family and those who want their bond to remain private in nature.

- On the sexual level: There is a radical difference in the relationship between a man and a woman with respect to a relationship between two persons of the same sex.

- As for the duration of the relationship: There is a difference between a temporary commitment, as in cohabitation, and a permanent commitment, as happens in marriage.

- On the level of the relationship between rights and duties: While marriage is firmly based on duties, in order to protect the vulnerable as much as possible, the new forms of cohabitation are centered more on rights.

- Between cohabitation and other relationships based on affection or solidarity (for example, forms of mutual assistance among elderly persons or religious who live together and support one another, or among grandparents and grandchildren who live together . . .). Why should cohabitants have preference? Because their relationship is based on sexual union? But if this is all that matters, then economic incentives would also have to be created for other sexual relationships, like polygamy, incest . . . And then, why only relationships between two persons, and not three, or four, or more?

✠ Moreover, granting a different status to spouses than to cohabitants is not discrimination. The relationship of spouses is different from that of cohabitants, because cohabitants, among other things, do not take on the responsibilities and obligations to which spouses commit themselves. It is not right to claim rights without accepting duties!

2. Pose serious problems on the legal level?

The legal recognition of cohabitation poses serious problems on the legal level in that

- It introduces a new legal issue, because the rights of cohabitants are recognized precisely in that they are cohabitants, since cohabitation is considered legally relevant for society.
- It distorts the very nature of law.
  - Law does not exist for the sake of giving legal form or ideological recognition to any sort of cohabitation whatsoever. Law has the purpose, in part, of guaranteeing public responses to social demands that go beyond the private dimension of existence.
  - Not every one of our desires or choices can or should be recognized by law, or even be given a status. Above all, it is not the subjective value of an interpersonal relationship that determines the level of protection that it should receive from the legal system, but its social value. The system does not protect a relationship only because it is perceived as significant by the subjects who are living in it, but because it holds value for all of society. For example, although friendship is one of the most supremely gratifying things for a person, and although it can even be stronger and more significant than some instances of cohabitation, it is not regulated by the law.

- Moreover, the emotional element escapes the observation of law: How is it measured? What criterion is used to evaluate its importance?
- It seems absurd and contradictory that the legal system should grant a status "de iuris" to cohabitants who wish to remain so only "de facto."

✠ Legal recognition of cohabitation would entail significant consequences in many areas, like those of adoption, education, labor rights, taxation, and economic assistance. And the consequences for religious organizations would directly impact the schools, hospitals, orphanages, and universities that they run.

✠ In any case, the stamp of legality, variously applied, does not turn wrong into right.

What must Catholic politicians do?

✠ In his recent post-synodal apostolic exhortation *Sacramentum Caritatis*, Pope Benedict XVI affirmed: "Catholic politicians and legislators, conscious of their grave responsibility before society, must feel particularly bound, on the basis of a properly formed conscience, to introduce and support laws inspired by values grounded in human nature," which include "the family built upon marriage between a man and a woman" (no. 83). "Bishops," he continues, "are bound to reaffirm constantly these values as part of their responsibility to the flock entrusted to them" (ibid.). It would therefore be inconsistent for a Christian to support the legal recognition of any form of nonmarital sexual relationship.

✠ The Christian believer is required to form his or her conscience by seriously consulting the teaching of the Magisterium, and therefore may not "appeal to the principle of pluralism or to the autonomy of lay involvement in political life to support policies affecting the common good which compromise or undermine fundamental ethical requirements" (*Doctrinal Note on Some Questions Regarding the Participation of Catholics in Political Life*, no. 5).

✠ In particular, one must keep in mind the specific statement of the CDF according to which, "when legislation in favor of the recognition of homosexual unions is proposed for the first time in a legislative assembly, the Catholic lawmaker has a moral duty to express his opposition clearly and publicly and to vote against it. To vote in favor of a law so harmful to the common good is gravely immoral" (*Considerations Regarding Proposals to Give Legal Recognition to Unions Between Homosexual Persons*, no. 10).

Why do the bishops intervene?

✠ The bishops have the right and duty to be the guardians of a truth and a wisdom that draw their origin from the Gospel, and continue to produce valuable fruits of love, faithfulness, and service of others, as so many families bear witness every day. And thus they have the responsibility of enlightening the consciences of believers, so that they may find the best way to embody the Christian vision of the human person and society in their everyday lives, personal and social, and to offer valid reasons that can be shared by all for the sake of the common good.

✠ The Church always has the family at heart and attentively supports it, being aware, together with very many others, including nonbelievers, of the value represented by the family for the growth of persons and of the whole society, for which the existence of the family is an irreplaceable resource. For this reason, it has always asked that lawmakers also promote and defend it.

✠ "If we tell ourselves that the Church ought not to interfere in such matters, we cannot but answer: are we not concerned with the human being? Do not believers, by virtue of the great culture of their faith, have the right to make a pronouncement on all this? Is it not their—our—duty to raise our voices to defend the human being, that creature who, precisely in the inseparable unity of body and spirit, is the image of God?" (Pope Benedict XVI, Christmas address to the members of the Roman Curia, December 22, 2006).

✠ We must be on guard "against the pragmatic attitude, widespread today, which systematically justifies compromise on essential human values, as if it were the inevitable acceptance of a lesser evil" (Pope Benedict XVI, Address, March 24, 2007).

✠ The bishops thus offer an opportunity to the consciences of all, and in particular to those responsible for making laws, to consider the consistent choices to be made and the future consequences of their decisions.

✠ The bishops do not have political interests to assert; they simply feel the duty of making their contribution to the common good, prompted above all by the requests of the many citizens who turn to them.

What commitment must every person make?

Each person must reaffirm, defend, and promote more and more the identity and uniqueness of marriage as the union of a man and a woman, with particular rights and duties.

Benedict XVI was absolutely correct in saying, "Here, it is not a question of specific norms of Catholic morals but of elementary truths that concern our common humanity: respecting them is essential for the good of the person and of society . . . It is a serious error to obscure the value and roles of the legitimate family founded on marriage by attributing legal recognition to other improper forms of union for which there is really no effective social need" (Address to politicians of the region, province, and city of Rome, January 12, 2006).

✠

For more on this topic, see the following pontifical documents:

Vatican Council II, *Gaudium et Spes,* nos. 47-50
Pope Paul VI, *Humanae Vitae,* 1968
Pope John Paul II, *Familiaris Consortio,* 1982; *Mulieris Dignitatem,* 1988
Pope Benedict XVI, *Deus Caritas Est,* LEV, 2006
Congregation for the Doctrine of the Faith, *Persona Humana,* 1975; *Letter to the Bishops of the Catholic Church on the Pastoral Care of Homosexual Persons,* October 1, 1986; *Donum Vitae,* 1988; *Considerations*

Regarding Proposals to Give Legal Recognition to Unions Between Homosexual Persons, June 3, 2003; *Letter to the Bishops of the Catholic Church on the Collaboration of Men and Women in the Church and in the World,* 2004

Catechism of the Catholic Church, nos. 337-350; 487-502; 1601-1666; 2331-2400, esp. 2357-2359; 2396

Compendium of the CCC, nos. 487-502

Congregation for Catholic Education, *Instruction Concerning the Criteria for the Discernment of Vocations with Regard to Persons with Homosexual Tendencies in View of Their Admission to the Seminary and to Holy Orders,* November 4, 2005

Pontifical Council for the Family, *The Truth and Meaning of Human Sexuality,* 1995

International Theological Commission, *Communion and Stewardship: Human Persons Created in the Image of God,* 2004, nos. 32-39

XV
Parenthood

What are the characteristics of human fatherhood and motherhood?

Human procreation

✠ Is an essential end of marriage between a man and a woman. In fact, conjugal love tends to be fecund by nature, since the conjugal act has two meanings: the unitive meaning (the total and definitive donation of the spouses to one another) and the procreative meaning (fruitful and open to the gift of life to a new human being).

✠ Reveals in a preeminent way the dignity of human beings, called to emulate the goodness and fecundity that descend from God, who through them continually expands and enriches the human family

✠ Although it is biologically similar to the generation of other beings in nature, has in itself, in an essential and exclusive way, a "likeness" with God: it is a particular form of the special participation of the spouses in the creative work of God. "Parents should regard as their proper mission the task of transmitting human life and educating those to whom it has been transmitted. They should realize that they are thereby cooperators with the love of God the Creator, and are, so to speak, the interpreters of that love" (*Gaudium et Spes*, no. 50).

✠ Expresses the social subjectivity of the family and awakens the dynamism of love and solidarity among the generations that lies at the basis of society, contributing to the communion of the generations

✠ Represents a task of nature that is not simply physical but spiritual. Through it, in fact, passes the genealogy of the person, which has its eternal beginning in God and must lead to him.

✠ Is the fruit of conjugal love (the total, definitive, and reciprocal donation between man and woman), which mirrors the eternally fecund love among the three divine Persons, and the gift of Christ to his Church, which becomes fecund in the rebirth of man, in Christ, through Baptism

How is conjugal fecundity, or fruitfulness, expressed?

It is expressed and actualized, in a complementary way, on the level of

✠ The couple (interpersonal fecundity): The spouses, day after day, should deepen their understanding of themselves and of each other, their mutual respect and love, their human and Christian growth.

✠ Physical-biological generation: The child, an extraordinarily precious gift of marriage

✠ The service of child raising (formational fecundity): By raising their children, the parents, who are primarily but not solely responsible for this, transmit the fruits of their moral, spiritual, and supernatural life.

✠ Human community (social fecundity): Helping society in the various forms of volunteer work

✠ Ecclesial community (apostolic fecundity): Commitment of witness and service in the Christian community

What is the significance of the conjugal act?

"The conjugal act has a twofold meaning: unitive (the mutual self-giving of the spouses) and procreative (an openness to the transmission of life). No one may break the inseparable connection which God has established between these two meanings of the conjugal act by excluding one or the other of them" (*Compendium of the* CCC, no. 496).

"If each of these essential qualities, the unitive and the procreative, is preserved, the use of marriage fully retains its sense of true mutual love and its ordination to the supreme responsibility of parenthood to which man is called" (*Humanae Vitae*, no. 12).

"Parents should regard as their proper mission the task of transmitting human life and educating those to whom it has been transmitted. They should realize that they are thereby cooperators with the love of God the Creator, and are, so to speak, the interpreters of that love. Thus they will fulfill their task with human and Christian responsibility" (*Gaudium et Spes*, no. 50).

How is responsibility realized in fatherhood and motherhood?

✠ It is realized

- Through the dedication and generosity of raising a large family
- Or, for good reason and with respect for the moral law, with the decision to avoid a new pregnancy either temporarily or for an undetermined period

✠ In both cases, the Christian spouses consider a fundamental question: Does our decision to give life to a new child or not correspond to the will of God? What does God want us to do about this, at this time?

How must the child be considered?

The child is

- A human being, created in the image and likeness of God
- A gift, the greatest gift of marriage:
  - The gift of self, on the part of the parents, to a new human being, the fruit of their total and definitive donation

- The gift of self, on the part of the child, to brothers, sisters, parents, the whole family. The child's life becomes a gift for the givers of life themselves.
- A living reflection and permanent sign of love, of conjugal unity. Today, unfortunately, rather than being seen as a gift of God welcomed within the loving intimacy of marriage between a man and a woman, the child is instead viewed as a mere human product.

Is there such thing as a right to have a child?

There is no such thing as a right to have a child. If there were, the child would be considered a possession, something to be consumed, the realization of a personal desire. If there were a "claim" on the child, the child would become a *product* to be consumed, instead of being a *gift* to be welcomed.

There is instead the right of the child to be the fruit of the specific act of the conjugal love of his or her parents, and also the right to be respected as a person from the moment of conception.

When is the regulation of conception moral?

When the spouses have valid reasons and use methods in keeping with morality. In their conduct, Christian spouses must remember that they may not simply do as they please but must always be guided by a conscience attuned to the divine law and docile to the Magisterium of the Church, which authentically interprets that law in the light of the Gospel.

What must the spouses take into account in living fatherhood and motherhood responsibly?

✠ The spouses must keep in mind

- Their own human condition (physical, emotional, spiritual, financial)
- The children already born or yet to be born
- Their own families
- Society
- A positive vision of life and an attitude of openness and service to it, including when, for serious reasons and in respect for the moral law, the spouses decide to avoid a new pregnancy temporarily or for an undetermined period of time
- Divine providence
- The conditions of life in their time, in both their material and spiritual aspects
- The scale of values and of the good of the family, temporal society, and the Church

✠ Their decision must therefore not be the fruit of egotism, nor must it be influenced by outside parties, much less by the public authorities.

Who has the right to decide on the interval between births and the number of children?

This right belongs only to the spouses. It is an inalienable right to be exercised before God, considering in a calm and deliberate manner their duties to one another, to their children, to the family and society.

What are the responsible means for regulating procreation?

✠ In the first place, the following must be rejected as morally illicit:

- Abortion, which is an abominable crime
- Direct sterilization
- The means of contraception in their different forms. To be excluded as intrinsically evil is "any action which either before, at the moment of, or after sexual intercourse, is specifically intended to prevent procreation—whether as an end or as a means" (*Humanae Vitae*, no. 14).

✠ The following are morally acceptable for just reasons:

- Periodic abstinence
- Recourse to the wife's infertile periods for the expression of the conjugal act

What is the difference between the morally licit and illicit means?

✠ "These two cases are completely different. In the former the married couple rightly use a faculty provided them by nature. In the latter they obstruct the natural development of the generative process. It cannot be denied that in each case the married couple, for acceptable reasons, are both perfectly clear in their intention to avoid children and wish to make sure that none will result. But it is equally true that it is exclusively in the former case that husband and wife are ready to abstain from intercourse during the fertile period as often as for reasonable motives the birth of another child is not desirable. And when the infertile period recurs, they use their married intimacy to express their mutual love and safeguard their fidelity toward one another. In doing this they certainly give proof of a true and authentic love" (*Humanae Vitae*, no. 16).

✠ The difference between natural methods and contraceptive methods is not "technical," but "ethical," meaning that it has to do with behavior. This is not simply a matter of acquiring and spreading scientific knowledge about the physiology of sexuality and about methods of diagnosing female fertility but of modifying one's behavior through abstinence.

Why is contraception illicit?

✠ Because by resorting to contraception the spouses separate the two meanings that God the Creator has inscribed in the being of man and woman and in the dynamism of their sexual communion: the unitive meaning and the procreative meaning. In this way, "they act as 'arbiters' of the divine plan and they 'manipulate' and degrade human sexuality—and with it themselves and their married partner—by altering its value of 'total' self-giving. Thus the innate language that expresses the total reciprocal self-giving of husband and wife is overlaid, through contraception, by an objectively contradictory language, namely, that of not giving oneself totally to the other. This leads not only to a positive refusal to be open to life but also to a falsification of the inner truth of conjugal love, which is called upon to give itself in personal totality" (*Familiaris Consortio*, no. 32).

✠ Contraception, and abortion even more so, has its roots in a mentality of hedonism and irresponsibility toward sexuality, and presupposes a selfish concept of freedom that sees procreation as an obstacle to the expression of one's own personality.

What serious consequences do artificial birth control methods cause?

Here are some of these serious consequences, which Paul VI indicates in *Humanae Vitae* (no.17):

✠ "Let them first consider how easily this course of action could open wide the way for marital infidelity and a general lowering of moral standards. Not much experience is needed to be fully aware of human weakness and to understand that human beings—and especially the young, who are so exposed to temptation—need incentives to keep the moral law, and it is an evil thing to make it easy for them to break that law.

✠ "Another effect that gives cause for alarm is that a man who grows accustomed to the use of contraceptive methods may forget the reverence due to a woman, and, disregarding her physical and emotional equilibrium, reduce her to being a mere instrument for the satisfaction of his own desires, no longer considering her as his partner whom he should surround with care and affection.

✠ "Finally, careful consideration should be given to the danger of this power passing into the hands of those public authorities who care little for the precepts of the moral law. Who will blame a government which in its attempt to resolve the problems affecting an entire country resorts to the same measures as are regarded as lawful by married people in the solution of a particular family difficulty? Who will prevent public authorities from favoring those contraceptive methods which they consider more effective?"

What is periodic abstinence?

✠ It is abstaining from conjugal relations during the periods of female fertility. Such abstinence, in these situations and for a certain time, in addition to the exercise of responsible parenthood, can also

- Be an authentic sign of love, attention, respect for the other
- Play an educational role. It can be good practice for acquiring marital chastity and respecting conjugal fidelity, including during periods of the temporary and/or prolonged absence of one's spouse, or during times of unreadiness or illness on the part of one or the other.

- Even offer a therapeutic service, promoting greater dedication and intensity of love in the conjugal act. Waiting can increase, purify, enrich, and perfect the desire for mutual self-donation and develop honest and chaste conjugal affection.

- Foster the knowledge and mastery of self in the spouses: "This self-discipline does demand that they persevere in their purpose and efforts, it has at the same time the salutary effect of enabling husband and wife to develop to their personalities and to be enriched with spiritual blessings. For it brings to family life abundant fruits of tranquility and peace. It helps in solving difficulties of other kinds. It fosters in husband and wife thoughtfulness and loving consideration for one another. It helps them to repel inordinate self-love, which is the opposite of charity. It arouses in them a consciousness of their responsibilities" (*Humanae Vitae*, no. 21).

✠ "A very valuable witness can and should be given by those husbands and wives who through the joint exercise of periodic continence have reached a more mature personal responsibility with regard to love and life. As Paul VI wrote: 'To them the Lord entrusts the task of making visible to people the holiness and sweetness of the law which unites the mutual love of husband and wife with their cooperation with the love of God, the author of human life'" (*Familiaris Consortio*, no. 35).

How can the periods of female fertility and infertility be determined?

✠ It is possible through the use of natural methods, based on the woman's observation of her body and her biological rhythm, and together with the simple observation of bodily rhythms, temperature, secretions, various signs and symptoms of fertility . . .

✠ These natural methods are based on two scientific truths:

- Biological (a woman's fertility is of limited duration)
- Sexological (the sexual act is not of itself always procreative)

What does the Church say about the natural methods for determining female fertility?

✠ The Church, although it does not adopt any particular method, holds that it is morally justified to resort, for valid reasons, to the natural methods through which one takes into account, for the use of matrimony, the natural rhythms of woman inherent in the procreative functions, and thus regulates the natural process without offending moral principles.

"When, instead, by means of recourse to periods of infertility, the couple respect the inseparable connection between the unitive and procreative meanings of human sexuality, they are acting as 'ministers' of God's plan and they 'benefit from' their sexuality according to the original dynamism of 'total' self-giving, without manipulation or alteration" (*Familiaris Consortio*, no. 32).

✠ Such natural methods are particularly useful, because they make it easier both to achieve pregnancy and to avoid it, by helping to identify the woman's fertile or infertile period.

✠ When one speaks of "natural" regulation, what is meant is not simply a respect of the biological rhythm. More comprehensively, it means responding to the truth of the person in his or her intimate unity of spirit, mind, and body, a unity that can never be reduced to a mere collection of biological mechanisms.

✠ "The methods of observation which enable the couple to determine the periods of fertility permit them to administer what the Creator has wisely inscribed in human nature without interfering with the integral significance of sexual giving. In this way spouses, respecting the full truth of their love, will be able to modulate its expression in conformity with these rhythms without taking anything from the totality of the gift of self that union in the flesh expresses. Obviously, this requires maturity in love which is not instantly acquired but involves dialogue and reciprocal listening, as well as a special mastery of the sexual impulse in a journey of growth in virtue" (Pope Benedict XVI, Message at the 40th anniversary of *Humanae Vitae*, October 2, 2008).

How are the natural methods taught?

✠ The centers of study and of teaching on these natural methods for regulating fertility, and also physicians, researchers, pastoral workers, and political authorities in their respective areas of competence, can provide valid assistance for responsible motherhood and fatherhood by

- Helping the spouses to know and appreciate these methods in their foundation and justification, as well as in their practical repercussions, and to apply them well in their concrete conditions
- Offering increasingly solid scientific bases for a regulation of conception that is respectful of the person and of God's plan for the human couple and for procreation
- Exploring this argument in its various aspects: biological, scientific, cultural, psycho-social, moral, spiritual, and formative
- Promoting at the same time the comprehensive education in moral values that recourse to such methods presupposes in regard to spouses, engaged couples, young people in general, and also social and pastoral workers
- Helping to dispel, in this area, stereotypes and misinformation, very often amplified by a certain financially motivated propaganda
- Fostering research programs in this field, and also in the formation of future professionals capable of helping young people and couples to make increasingly deliberate and responsible decisions

✠ In recent years, thanks to contributions from countless Christian couples all over the world, the natural methods have entered into the experience and reflection of family groups and movements and human and ecclesial associations. Couples that use natural methods help to bear witness to the practicability, efficacy, and relevance of a scientific method that is beneficial for human beings.

✠ It is more necessary than ever to help couples to understand that, in order to determine the periods of fertility, the natural methods are the safest, the healthiest, the most economical, the simplest, and the most moral.

What are the positive aspects of the natural methods?

✠ From a human point of view, they permit spouses to

- Respect each other's bodies and the biological laws inscribed in their person
- Achieve pregnancy, or avoid it for valid reasons
- Pursue interpersonal responsibility, communication, and tenderness
- Learn authentic freedom
- Govern the tendencies of instinct and passion

✠ From the point of view of Christian morality, the natural methods permit spouses to

- Recognize that the procreative capacity is a reflection of the creative communion of Trinitarian love, a cooperation with the creative power of God, source and Father of every life: the spouses are collaborators and ministers, not masters of human life

- Be faithful to God's plan for spousal, sacramental love
- Respect the laws inscribed by God in the natural, essential structure of the person
- Avoid the moral evil of other, illicit methods

What can spouses do when they do not have children?

✠ They can resort above all to medicine, seeking to resolve their problems in a way respectful of the dignity of the person.

✠ They can demonstrate their generosity and their spiritual, social, and ecclesial fecundity by

- Adopting abandoned children
- Taking in foster children
- Doing volunteer work

In *Familiaris Consortio*, John Paul II emphasizes that "even when procreation is not possible, conjugal life does not for this reason lose its value. Physical sterility in fact can be for spouses the occasion for other important services to the life of the human person, for example, adoption, various forms of educational work, and assistance to other families and to poor or handicapped children" (no. 14).

✠

For more on this topic, see the following pontifical documents:

Pope Paul VI, *Humanae Vitae*, 1968
Pope John Paul II, *Familiaris Consortio*, 1981
Catechism of the Catholic Church, nos. 2362-2400
Compendium of the CCC, nos. 495-502

XVI
Irregular
Situations

What are irregular affective situations?

✠ They are

- Cohabitation
- Civil marriage alone
- Divorced and cohabiting or remarried civilly

✠ In this section, such persons will be referred to more briefly as those who are living in irregular situations.

✠ It must be clarified that there is no intention here of taking into consideration the subjective moral evaluation of the individual person (*de internis Ecclesia non iudicat*), but only the objective moral situation of grave sin of those living in one of the situations described above.

✠ Those who are separated while remaining faithful to their religious marriage are not in an irregular affective situation.

Why is separation not to be considered an irregular situation?

Because, in separation, the fidelity and indissolubility of the Sacrament of Matrimony is maintained.

✠ There can be "situations in which living together becomes practically impossible for a variety of reasons. In such cases the Church permits the physical *separation* of the couple and their living apart. The spouses do not cease to be husband and wife before God and so are not free to contract a new union. In this difficult situation, the best solution would be, if possible, reconciliation. The Christian community is called to help these persons live out their situation in a Christian manner and in fidelity to their marriage bond which remains indissoluble" (CCC, no. 1649).

✠ Even in the case of the separation of the spouses, they must always provide sufficient support and education for their children.

✠ The Church accepts separation in some cases as a means to overcome the difficulties of the couple, and therefore as a temporary *modus vivendi* in view of a recomposition of the conjugal and familial union.

Can those who are living in irregular situations receive absolution in the Sacrament of Confession or receive Holy Communion?

No.

✠ They cannot receive Holy Communion, because their objective irregular situation prevents them, being gravely contrary to the teaching of Christ. This is not a matter of punishment or discrimination, nor of an undue imposition on the part of Church authority. It is simply a matter of

- Absolute fidelity to the will of Christ, who has again entrusted to us the indissolubility of marriage as a gift of the Creator
- Respect for Eucharistic Communion, which requires consistency in the life decisions of those who receive it. There is no *right* to Communion, which is primarily a gift from God and must be received by those who are at least without mortal sin.
- The objective and real limitation of the belonging of these persons in the ecclesial community: they find themselves in an ecclesially and Eucharistically dissonant situation.

The Church takes note of an objective irregular situation that does not permit one to receive the Eucharist and leaves the judgment of guilt to God. "They are unable to be admitted thereto from the fact that their state and condition of life objectively contradict that union of love between Christ and the Church which is signified and effected by the Eucharist" (*Familiaris Consortio*, no. 84).

"Consequently, they cannot receive Eucharistic communion as long as this situation persists. For the same reason, they cannot exercise certain ecclesial responsibilities" (CCC, no. 1650), for example being godparents or sponsors in the celebration of the Sacraments of Baptism and Confirmation.

✠ There is another special pastoral reason: if these persons were admitted to Eucharistic Communion, the faithful would be led into error and confusion about the doctrine of the Church on the sacramental and indissoluble nature of marriage.

Is Holy Communion not permitted in any case at all?

✠ Access to Holy Communion is opened only by sacramental absolution, which can be given only to those who, repentant over having violated the teaching of Christ, are sincerely disposed to a way of life that is no longer in contradiction with the essential characteristics of the Sacrament of Matrimony.

✠ Whenever the man and woman cannot separate for serious reasons—for example, the need to raise their children—they can make the commitment of living in complete continence, as brother and sister, abstaining from conjugal sexual relations. In this case, they can receive Eucharistic Holy Communion, although they are still required to avoid giving scandal (for example, by receiving Holy Communion at a church where they are not known).

Since they cannot receive Holy Communion, are they also excluded from the love of Christ and of the Church?

Of course not!

✠ Those who live in an irregular situation continue to be loved by Christ, they are still members of the Church, they can and must participate in its life, even though they are unable to receive Eucharistic Communion and the Sacrament of Penance.

✠ A Eucharist without immediate sacramental Communion is certainly not complete, it lacks something essential. Nonetheless, it is also true that participating in the Eucharist without Eucharistic Communion is not nothing; it is still a form of contact with its mystery.

✠ In that they perceive as pain and suffering their breaking of Christ's request concerning the sacramentality of the love between a man and a woman and/or the indissolubility of this bond, and therefore the inability to have full communion in the sacraments of the Church

- They can feel embraced by the crucified Lord, be closer to the Lord who suffered for us and suffers with us. Their burden is not easy and light in the sense of being small or insignificant, but it becomes light because the Lord—and the whole Church together with him—shares in it.
- They can trust in the mercy of God
- They "find a saving power and effectiveness in a Communion of desire and from participation at the

Eucharist" (Pope Benedict XVI, Closing homily at the 49th International Eucharistic Conference, June 22, 2008)

- They also offer a positive witness to other believers: with their suffering, they help us to understand that suffering can be a very positive reality, that it urges us to mature, to become more fully ourselves, closer to the Lord. It must not be forgotten, in fact, that every marriage that breaks up brings tension, stress, pain, inner confusion, emotional and practical problems, and wounds.

✠ They can participate in the life of the ecclesial community in various ways.

How can those living in an irregular situation still participate in the life of the Church?

✠ They not only can, but as baptized persons, they have the right and the duty to participate in various aspects of the Church's life, such as

- Persevering in prayer—personal, conjugal, familial
- Listening to the Word of God
- Attending the Sacrifice of the Mass, also making what is called "spiritual Communion"
- Cultivating the spirit and works of penance, in order to implore God's grace day by day
- Engaging in works of charity and in community initiatives on behalf of justice
- Raising the children in the Christian faith

✠ In this way, they understand and manifest that their participation in the life of the Church cannot be reduced exclusively to the reception of the Eucharist.

What is meant by the nullity of the Sacrament of Matrimony?

✠ In the first place, the customary reference to the "annulment" of the sacramental bond of marriage is incorrect. The precise term is "nullity." The Church can only declare that sacrament null, or never realized, in that it was ruined at its origin by elements so important as to be considered fundamental for the validity of marriage itself. If these elements are lacking, the marriage is null *ab origine*, and with retroactive effects. Thus a valid marriage, celebrated in church, *lasts forever*: it either is or it isn't.

✠ In cases that are concluded with the declaration of nullity, what God has united is not divided. The Church maintains, out of fidelity to the words of Jesus ("Whoever divorces his wife and marries another commits adultery against her; and if she divorces her husband and marries another, she commits adultery" [Mk 10:11-12]), that a new union cannot be recognized as valid if the first marriage was valid. For the Church, when marriage is celebrated validly, it is indissoluble (see the section "Marriage and Family").

✠ The declaration of nullity certifies that the marriage never existed and is therefore much different from divorce, which simply declares that the marriage, at the civil level, is finished. In the declaration of nullity, instead, there is no dissolution of a bond, but only the ascertainment of whether this bond existed validly in the first place.

✠ The canonical process of matrimonial nullity constitutes "a means of ascertaining the truth about the conjugal bond. Thus, their constitutive aim is not to complicate the life of the faithful uselessly, nor far less to exacerbate their litigation, but rather to render a service to the truth" (Pope Benedict XVI, Address to members of the Roman Rota, January 28, 2006).

What can the causes of this nullity be?

✠ The essential elements for the validity of a marriage between a man and a woman are unity, fidelity, indissolubility, openness to fecundity, and the good of the spouses. If one of the two parties rules out with a positive act of the will, on the occasion of the celebration of the marriage (and not afterward), even one of the aforementioned essential elements, the consent is considered to be ruined, so the marriage never took place.

✠ There can therefore be various causes of the nullity of a marriage celebrated in church (see *Code of Canon Law* [CIC], cc. 1093-1102), and in some cases they can be complementary. The main causes are

- Lack of the adequate use of reason
- Grave lack of critical evaluation of marital rights and duties

- The inability to take on the essential obligations of marriage for psychological reasons
- Ignorance of the essence of marriage
- An error about the person or one of the essential qualities of the spouse
- Having concealed from the other person by deceit, for the sake of extorting his or her consent, a vice or serious disease (for example, AIDS, homosexuality, sterility, cancer . . .), which by its nature could seriously disturb the communion of conjugal life
- The exclusion of the sacramental nature of marriage or of one of its essential properties (fidelity, the indissolubility of the bond) or of one of its purposes (the good of the spouses, the generation and education of children)
- The stipulation of a future condition
- Violence or grave fear caused from the outside (which one can escape only by agreeing to marriage)

✠ To these causes of nullity are added the diriment impediments (CIC, cc. 1068-1076), like

- Impotence
- Lack of sufficient age, or sixteen years for the man and fourteen for the woman
- Consanguinity
- Major sacred orders or perpetual religious vows
- Disparity of worship

A dispensation can be obtained for some of these impediments.

✠ Sterility is not an impediment to marriage.

✠ Before the celebration of a marriage, all of the faithful are obliged to reveal to the pastor or to the local ordinary any impediments of which they are aware with regard to the future spouses (see CIC, c. 1067).

What is the procedure to be followed in cases of nullity?

✠ In the first place, it is more appropriate than ever to verify with a priest the grounds for a claim of nullity for one's marriage.

✠ Once the claim is substantiated, one must go to the diocesan tribunal, presenting the necessary documentation.

✠ In order to introduce a case of nullity, it is necessary that

- The spouses no longer be living under the same roof, that there is at least a de facto separation
- In addition to well-informed witnesses, a lawyer also be consulted. This cannot be an ordinary lawyer, but a properly qualified lawyer who can be
  - Chosen from an official registry, in which case the interested party must pay, or
  - Requested from the tribunal, in which case the expense may be compensated in full or in part, if the person pursuing the claim is in financial hardship

✠ About the levels of judgment: Two levels of judgment are necessary for the declaration of nullity—the first tribunal and the appellate tribunal.

✠ About the process of judgment: After the initial finding, the case goes to appeal, where three other judges examine the proceedings. If the initial finding is affirmed, the marriage is declared null, and the parties can get married in the Church. If the second finding is negative, then there must be a third level of judgment at the tribunal of the "Sacred Rota," now called the "Apostolic Tribunal of the Roman Rota," which is located in Rome.

✠ About the duration of the case: The first and second level of judgment generally take about three years.

✠ About privacy: The process is private. This means that no one can have access to the proceedings of the case, except for the interested parties, through their attorneys. No one can attend the hearings except for the attorneys. All of the employees of the tribunal are required to observe the privacy of marriage cases.

✠ About children, if applicable: The finding of nullity does not at all change the legal status of the children already born, who do not lose any rights (of inheritance or of any other kind). It is as if, for them, the marriage of their parents were valid in any case.

✠ About civil effects: The finding of nullity handed down by the ecclesiastical tribunal must be recognized as valid in the civil system. If it is recognized as valid, the marriage is also null for the state, and the former spouses are again recognized as unmarried.

Can those who lived in an irregular situation have a church funeral?

In this regard, the following must be taken into account:

✠ There is a right to a church funeral for all of the faithful departed (see CIC, c. 1176 §1), as long as they have not been legitimately deprived of this right (legitimately means on the basis of the provisions of the CIC, c. 1184).

✠ Now, applying what canon 1184 says regarding irregular situations, the deceased cannot be granted a religious funeral when three conditions are in place at the same time:

1. The irregular situation is displayed publicly (in the external forum).
2. The sinner, before death, gave no sign of repentance.
3. The celebration of the church funeral is a source of public scandal for the faithful (meaning that it encourages them to commit sin, in this case that of accepting the irregular situation).

✠ If a sign of repentance was shown

  ■ The church funeral is granted
  ■ It would be appropriate for the priest, during the funeral, to make some reference to this repentance, in order to remove the risk of scandal among the faithful, and

invite them to implore the mercy of God on behalf of the deceased, in addition to invoking Christian consolation on behalf of the grieving relatives

✠ A sign of repentance can be, for example

- During the person's life: having persevered in religious practice, being concerned with the Christian formation of the children, if any, etc.
- Before death: welcoming a priest, asking for the Sacrament of Confession and/or the Anointing of the Sick, agreeing to pray, kissing the crucifix, asking God for forgiveness in an apparent way, etc.

✠ In case of doubt, both about the sign of repentance and about whether or not scandal is given, the ultimate judgment belongs to the local ordinary, the bishop (see CIC, c. 1184 §2).

✠ When, in certain cases, the Church does not grant a religious funeral, it is because it wants to

- Respect the will of the person who, because of a conscious decision or as a result of his or her gravely immoral behavior, has separated himself or herself from the Church, from communion with it. This is why the Church does not impose a rite on the person who does not want one. The free decision of the person not to belong to the Church, manifested either expressly or implicitly through conduct of life clearly contrary to the Christian faith, must be respected even in opposition to the wishes of relatives.

- Stigmatize the objective immorality of certain states of life in which a believer might find himself or herself at the moment of death, as is precisely the case of those who find themselves in irregular situations
- Avoid a grave and widespread danger of scandal, of relativism, of indifference among the people

✠

For more on this topic, see the following pontifical documents:

Catechism of the Catholic Church, nos. 1601-1666; 1680-1690; 2331-2400

Compendium of the CCC, nos. 337-350; 354-356; 487-502

Code of Canon Law, cc. 1068-1076; 1093-1102

Pope John Paul II, *Familiaris Consortio*, 1982

Congregation for the Doctrine of the Faith, *Letter to the Bishops of the Catholic Church Concerning the Reception of Holy Communion by the Divorced and Remarried Members of the Faithful*, 1994